Easy Wok Cookbook for Beginners

100 Classic Chinese Recipes to Stir-Fry with Sizzling Success

Noby Veam

Table of Contents

Introduction

Busy schedules, hungry kids, and working adults make the efficiency of stir-fry a go-to choice for daily meals. It's also a crowd-pleaser for easy entertaining. With a wok and some preparation, it's possible to prepare multiple entrees for a houseful of guests while accommodating dietary preferences for omnivores, vegans, and others. In this book, I'll teach you what you need to know so that you can enjoy this fast and flavorful cooking method at home.

Although stir-frying was invented in China over 2,000 years ago, this ancient method of cooking is still widely used today. Creating flavorful, healthy one-pot meals in 30 minutes or less fits in well with the desire to simplify our lives. Moreover, stir-fry recipes use animal proteins such as meat, poultry, and seafood as just one of several ingredients. This greater focus on vegetables aligns with the recommendations from today's medical and nutritional professionals to eat more plant-based whole foods. Because of China's historic need to maximize resources, stir-frying's tools and techniques have evolved over thousands of years to make the most of fuel, space, and ingredients while ensuring the tastiest and most satisfying results in the shortest amount of time.

Since stir-frying originated in China, most of the recipes in this book are based on common Chinese ingredients, many of which are available in the produce section of grocery stores. You can also look for these items in the international aisle of your local market, at Asian markets, and online. Over the course of 2,000-plus years, stir-frying has spread well beyond China, so I've also included some recipes with interesting ingredients and flavors from other countries and cuisines.

I'll also take you step by step through the process and method of stir-frying itself. If you take a few extra minutes to read and practice the contents of the next chapter, you'll be creating your own quick and tasty signature stir-fry dishes in no time. So, let's get started!

CHINESE HOME COOKING FOR ALL

Welcome to your wok cooking adventure! Whether you are hoping to acquire new wok skills or to learn how to make your favorite Chinese restaurant dishes, we are here to help. In this chapter, we'll cover the history of Chinese food and wok cooking. We'll tell you how to choose the right wok and how to take care of it, and we'll explain wok cooking techniques and provide troubleshooting tips.

A Brief History of Chinese Food and Wok Cooking

Chinese cuisine has many regional sub-cuisines. The more inland regions of Sichuan and Hunan, for example, have hot, spicy flavors, whereas coastal regions such as Guangzhou and Shanghai have milder flavors. What unites the cuisines of these regions is use of the wok as one of the primary cooking vessels.

Chinese wok dishes are uniquely well suited to cooking at home because many evolved from the need to make a few ingredients stretch far and to use up small quantities of food. In fact, stir-frying makes the most out of small pieces of protein. A thinly sliced 6-ounce piece of beef, for example, takes very little time to cook, and when added to a variety of stir-fried vegetables, it can comfortably feed as many as four people.

The practicality of wok cooking led to the creation of Chinese-American takeout favorites. Egg foo yong, General Tso's chicken, moo shu pork, and fried rice were born out of Chinese immigrants' attempts to recreate the tastes of home utilizing locally available ingredients and to adapt them to draw customers to their restaurants.

All over the world, Chinese immigrants have adapted traditional Chinese dishes to local food and taste preferences to create fusion gems such as Singaporean rice noodles (stir-fried rice noodles with Chinese barbecue pork and curry powder) and Peruvian lomo saltado (sliced beef and tomatoes stir-fried with French fries and onions).

KNOW YOUR WOK

There are many different types of woks, and tasty food can be made in all of them. Still, it's important to know the pros and cons of each so you know what you're working with and can make the most of the wok you have.

Carbon-Steel Woks

Carbon-steel woks are the woks used in restaurants and many Chinese homes. Made from cold forged carbon steel, they are extremely durable if taken care of properly, and they are also the most inexpensive woks on the market. Carbon steel is an excellent heat conductor and is ideal for achieving wok hei.

Like cast-iron skillets, carbon-steel woks must be washed by hand, dried over heat, and oiled after each use to keep them from rusting. A well-seasoned carbon-steel wok develops a black patina over time and becomes essentially nonstick.

For stir-frying and deep-frying, we find the carbon-steel wok to be the best type of wok. If your budget allows, however, we suggest having another wok or pan designated for steaming and braising because the moisture can ruin the patina you've worked so hard to build up in your carbon-steel wok. You can certainly use your carbon-steel wok for all your wok cooking; it just requires a little extra care after you have cooked with moist-cooking methods.

We recommend carbon-steel woks for home cooks who will be using their wok quite a lot because frequent cooking helps maintain the wok's nonstick patina. Compared with stainless-steel and nonstick woks, carbon-steel woks require a little extra care, but you can't go wrong with their combination of low cost, excellent heat conduction, and durability.

Cast-Iron Woks

A Chinese cast-iron wok is thinner and lighter than American and European cast-iron pans, but still heavier than carbon-steel woks. Chinese cast-iron woks are usually found in Chinese or Asian specialty stores and can be used over gas, electric, or induction stove tops.

Cast-iron woks are great for deep-frying and steaming because they are heavier than carbon-steel woks and can retain heat longer. However, like carbon-steel woks, they require extra work to maintain their seasoning and to prevent rusting.

Stainless-Steel Woks

Stainless-steel woks are also great conductors of heat, and they require no seasoning or special maintenance. All you need to do is thoroughly clean them with soap and water as you would any other stainless-steel pan to avoid buildup. These woks are perfect for braising and steaming in addition to stir-frying because you don't have to worry about rust and water damage. However, you may find that you need a little more cooking oil when using a stainless-steel wok. Stainless-steel woks can be used over gas, electric, or induction stove tops.

Nonstick Woks

Nonstick woks are the new kids on the block. Their advantages are that they don't rust or need to be seasoned. They are great for cooks who use their woks infrequently because they are easy to clean and don't require constant maintenance. Nonstick woks can, however, be pricey. Because wok cooking is all about high heat, we recommend only high-quality non-Teflon/noncoated nonstick woks that are meant to be used over high heat. Wok hei cannot be fully achieved with a nonstick wok, but if your goal is to reduce the amount of oil used in stir-frying, this wok is for you. Be sure to use wooden or silicone utensils so as not to damage the nonstick surface. Most nonstick woks can be used over gas, electric, or induction stove tops (check manufacturer's recommendations to be sure).

Electric Woks

Live in a dorm? Boat? RV? The electric wok is the wok for you! You can't beat an electric wok for portability and versatility. The major drawback to using an electric wok for stir-frying is it just doesn't get hot enough. Electric woks are usually nonstick, so they are easy to clean as you would any other nonstick pan. Make sure to use wooden or silicone utensils so you don't scratch the wok interior. Electric woks cannot be immersed in water, so be careful not to get the electrical components wet.

Shape and Size Matter

Carbon-steel and cast-iron woks are available in both flat- and round-bottomed versions, whereas nonstick and stainless-steel woks are typically only flat-bottomed.

Flat-bottomed woks can rest on the stove top without tipping over. Round-bottomed woks need a wok ring to keep them stable. Flat-bottomed woks allow for more even heating than round-bottomed woks. Round-bottomed woks are used exclusively over a gas burner. A flat-bottomed wok is suitable for electric and gas stove tops; it is also the only wok that works with induction stove tops.

We recommend a 12-inch wok if you are cooking for 2 to 4 people, or a 14-inch wok if you're cooking for 4 to 6 people. We do not recommend using a wok larger than 14 inches at home because it is impossible to get a strong enough flame to properly heat a wok of that size.

Size is important, because if you overcrowd your wok, your food will steam and become soggy instead of stir-frying to perfection. If your wok is small or if you are cooking for a crowd, cook in batches so you can ensure that your food is in direct contact with the hot bottom and side of the wok.

SEASONING YOUR WOK

Unlike electric, nonstick, and stainless-steel woks, carbon-steel and cast-iron woks require seasoning, or the building up of a black patina, with each use. This patina eventually creates a nonstick surface and protects your wok from rusting.

Here are the four steps for removing the manufacturer's coating on a new wok and seasoning it:

1. Scrub the wok both inside and out with a scrubby pad with dish soap and hot water. Rinse and dry the wok with a dish towel.
2. Place the wok over a medium flame to completely dry the wok. When the wok is hot, turn off the heat and, using a folded paper towel held with kitchen tongs, rub a teaspoon of vegetable oil all over the inside of the wok. Allow the wok to cool, then wipe away the excess oil with a dry paper towel.
3. Return the wok to medium-high heat until a drop of water sizzles and evaporates on contact. Pour in 3 tablespoons oil and swirl to coat the base of the wok. Add a handful of unpeeled ginger slices and let them sizzle in the oil for about 30 seconds, swirling gently. Reduce the heat to medium and add a handful of peeled garlic cloves and toss the ginger and garlic until aromatic. This technique will help remove the new wok's

metallic taste. Turn off the heat, discard the oil and aromatics, and allow the wok to cool completely before rinsing it with hot water and drying it with a dish towel.

4. Place the wok over a medium flame. When the wok is hot, turn off the heat, and using a folded paper towel held with kitchen tongs, rub another teaspoon of vegetable oil all over the inside. Allow the wok to cool, then wipe away the excess oil with a dry paper towel. Woohoo! Your new wok is ready to use.

Easy Cooking with Your Wok

The wok is a super versatile pan that can cook just about anything. Most of this book's recipes are stir-fries, because stir-frying is one of the main ways to cook in a wok. However, some recipes in this book use other techniques, including deep-frying, steaming, and simmering.

Types of Stir-fry

Did you know that there's more than one way to stir-fry? There are, in fact, four major techniques:

Dry stir-fry. Dry stir-frying means stir-frying without the use of liquid other than a small amount of oil, and sometimes a bit of soy sauce or Shaoxing rice wine. Essentially, there is no sauce.

Wet stir-fry. Wet stir-frying is the opposite of dry stir-frying—wet stir-fries use liquid, usually rice wine, stock, or a sauce of some kind.

Clear stir-fry. Clear stir-frying allows a single ingredient to be the star of the show. Oil, salt, and a hot wok are the only items needed to bring out the best in a seasonal vegetable or a protein.

Velveting. Velveting is coating an ingredient (usually a delicate protein such as fish, shellfish, or chicken) in egg white and cornstarch before stir-frying it or before poaching it or briefly oil frying it prior to combining it with other ingredients for serving. Foods that have been velveted turn out tender and juicy.

Steaming, Simmering, and Other Ways to Rock Your Wok

The wok's versatility doesn't end with stir-frying. Steaming is probably the second-most popular way to use your wok. You'll need an expandable metal basket and a lid or stackable bamboo steamer baskets. If you get the stackable bamboo steamers, you can simultaneously cook several dishes in just one pan.

Woks can also be used for simmering soups, stews, and porridges and for braising meats and vegetables—that is, cooking them in small amounts of liquid in a shallow vessel. You don't need any special equipment to use your wok for simmering or braising; it is helpful, however, to have a snugly fitting cover for your wok to reduce liquid loss through evaporation. The wok's flared shape makes liquids evaporate relatively quickly.

Woks can also be used for deep-frying. A deep-fry thermometer is handy to have, but you can use our kitchen hack to determine when the oil is at the right temperature. Simply dip the handle of a wooden spoon into the oil heating up in your wok. If it bubbles and sizzles around the handle, the oil is sufficiently hot. If not, test it again in 20 seconds. Make sure to add your ingredients a few pieces at a time and deep-fry them in batches, because if you overcrowd the wok the oil can bubble out of it.

Wok This Way: 10 Steps to Stir-Fry Success

Here are our tips and tricks for stir-frying:

1. **Prep and measure everything before you start cooking.** Slice and marinate your proteins, cut your veggies, and mix up your sauces before you even turn on the stove. Line them up next to the stove in the order they will be cooked. Wok cooking is fast! You won't have time for prepping once you start cooking, so do it all before you turn on the heat.
2. **Get the wok hot.** For stir-frying, heat your wok over medium-high heat until a drop of water sizzles and evaporates on contact—if there's no sizzle, your wok is not hot enough. Make sure your wok is completely dry before moving on to the next step.
3. **Use a high-smoke-point oil.** For stir-frying, it's important to use an oil that will not burn at high temperatures, like vegetable, grapeseed, and avocado. Steer clear of extra-virgin olive oil, which will burn and smoke over high heat. Sesame oil should be added only at the end because it will burn if used at the beginning when your wok is at its hottest. Pour in the oil, then swirl it around to coat the bottom of the wok.
4. **Season the oil.** Season the oil by adding the aromatics—ginger and a pinch of salt first, then garlic if you're using it. Seasoning the oil leads to balanced, nuanced flavors and is a must in our book. Pay close attention, so you don't burn the aromatics.
5. **Your wok spatula is your best friend!** Use it to scoop, toss, and flip what you are cooking.
6. **Cook ingredients in the proper order.** Cook the protein first and transfer it to a bowl. Then cook the vegetables, adding the hardest to the wok first and the softest last. Hard and dense vegetables take longer to cook than soft, delicate vegetables. Once all the vegetables are crisp, return the protein to the pan and add the sauce.
7. **Add the sauce around the outside edge of the pan.** This technique helps prevent heat loss from the wok. As you add the sauce, toss the ingredients in it.
8. **Taste at the end and add a bright garnish.** Once all the ingredients have been incorporated into the sauce, give it a taste! Adjust seasoning with salt and pepper as needed. Adding a fresh garnish like thinly sliced scallions or cilantro makes your finished dish visually appealing.
9. **Cook in batches for a crowd.** Don't overload your wok. When you fill a wok to the brim, your ingredients will steam rather than stir-fry.
10. **Follow the recipes but use them as a road map.** Once you have the basics down, add your own twists and cater to your personal preferences. Have fun!

CLEANING AND STORING YOUR WOK

Step away from the dishwasher! Although it's tempting to throw a wok in the dishwasher, all woks should be washed by hand with a nonabrasive scrubby using soap and hot water. Contrary to myth, you can use a small amount of soap when cleaning carbon steel and cast iron, but too much soap can strip away the seasoned patina you've worked so hard to build up. Stainless-steel and nonstick woks can be dried with a kitchen towel and then put away.

It's important to clean your cast-iron or carbon-steel wok right away after the meal. Then give it a light seasoning. After washing your wok, follow step 4 in Seasoning Your Wok.

You can stack your wok with your other pots and pans in a cabinet as long as you slip a paper grocery bag or paper towels above and below it. Alternatively, hang your wok from a pot rack.

Troubleshooting Common Wok Problems

Q.Why is my stir-fry so soggy?

A.Using wet vegetables, overcrowding the wok, or both are the typical reasons for a soggy stir-fry. Make sure you're drying your vegetables properly (a salad spinner works great for leafy vegetables). And don't add too much food to the wok at once. If you need to double the recipe, make the dish twice (or make two different stir-fries for variety!) to avoid sogginess.

Q.How do I prevent meat from sticking to my wok?

A.A common mistake beginners make is not heating up the wok properly before adding the oil and not heating the oil up properly before adding the meat. Best practice is to heat the wok over medium-high heat until faint wisps of smoke appear. Then add the oil and swirl gently. As soon as you see the oil starting to smoke, add the meat. If the meat sticks—and it might—just let it sit against the hot wok for a few moments before lifting it up. Proteins need to develop a seared crust before they naturally stop sticking to the pan.

Q.What do I do if I see rust on my wok?

A.Don't panic! A little surface rust is a natural occurrence, especially if the wok hasn't been dried properly after being washed. Simply rewash the wok and gently scrub off the rust. Rinse it under hot water and dry it thoroughly by placing it on the stove over medium-high heat. Once the wok is hot and dry, turn off the heat and reseason it by following step 4 of Seasoning Your Wok.

Q.What's the best way to get stuck bits of food off my wok when cleaning?

A.Stuck-on food will come off more easily when the wok is still hot and hot water is poured in. Let the water sit for a few moments, then use the wok spatula to gently scrape off the stuck-on food. The food should come off easily as long as the wok is still hot.

Q.Not all of my vegetables are cooked through. Help!

A.If vegetables seem raw, stir-fry them for a couple minutes longer. You can also pop the lid onto the wok for a few minutes, then remove the lid and increase the heat to high and stir-fry to keep the vegetables moving until all the collected liquid from the steam condensation has evaporated.

VEGETABLES AND TOFU

Bok Choy with Sweet Red Pepper

SERVES 4 ; PREP TIME: 10 MINUTES ; COOK TIME: 5 MINUTES

This is a super-fast vegetable stir-fry that takes advantage of how quickly tender, fresh ingredients can be seared in a hot wok. Hoisin sauce is a thick sweet-and-salty glaze made from pureed fruit and soy sauce. It is also known as Cantonese barbecue sauce. You can find it in the international section of most grocery stores, You can also whip up your own version by combining 1 part soy sauce and 3 parts ketchup. If you want to add a protein, I recommend crispy extra-firm tofu (see here) with this dish.

2 tablespoons cooking oil

4 garlic cloves, crushed and chopped

1 tablespoon crushed and chopped ginger

2 cups red bell peppers, cut into 1-inch pieces

1 (15-ounce) can straw mushrooms, drained and rinsed

2 cups bok choy, cut diagonally into 1-inch pieces

¼ cup hoisin sauce

4 scallions, cut diagonally into ¼-inch pieces

Rice or noodles, for serving

1. In a wok, heat the cooking oil over high heat until it begins to smoke.
2. Add the garlic, ginger, and bell peppers to the wok and stir-fry for 1 minute.
3. Add the straw mushrooms and stir-fry for 1 minute.
4. Toss in the bok choy and hoisin sauce and stir-fry for 1 minute.
5. Add the scallions and toss well, before serving over rice or noodles.

VARIATION TIP: If you want to add some heat to this dish, you can substitute chile peppers in place of the bell peppers. Poblano peppers are a little hotter, jalapeños are hotter still, and bird's eye peppers are really hot. You can also add 1 teaspoon of spicy sesame oil in step 4 for additional flavor and heat.

King Oyster Mushrooms and Broccoli with Bamboo Shoots

SERVES 4 ; PREP TIME: 15 MINUTES ; COOK TIME: 5 MINUTES

King oyster mushrooms are firm, meaty mushrooms, also known as king trumpet mushrooms. They have thick cylindrical stalks and comparatively small caps. The stalks can be as much as 4 or 5 inches long and 1 inch or more across, making them perfect for cutting into medallions for cooking. I think of sliced king oyster mushrooms as a vegetarian version of sea scallops, which is what they look like in this recipe.

2 tablespoons cooking oil

4 garlic cloves, crushed and chopped

1 tablespoon crushed and chopped ginger

8 ounces king oyster mushrooms, cut into ½-inch coins

2 cups broccoli florets (1 inch wide)

2 tablespoons soy sauce

1 tablespoon Shaoxing rice wine

¼ cup hoisin sauce

1 (8-ounce) can bamboo shoots, drained and rinsed

4 scallions, cut diagonally into ¼-inch pieces

Rice or noodles, for serving

1. In a wok, heat the cooking oil over high heat until it begins to smoke.
2. Add the garlic, ginger, and mushrooms to the wok and stir-fry for 1 minute.
3. Add the broccoli and stir-fry for 2 minutes.
4. Add the soy sauce, wine, hoisin sauce, and bamboo shoots and stir-fry for 1 minute.
5. Add the scallions, toss well, and serve immediately over rice or noodles.

Stir-Fried Lettuce with Oyster Sauce

SERVES 4 TO 6 ; PREP TIME: 5 MINUTES ; COOK TIME: 10 MINUTES

Raw vegetables are rarely served in Chinese cuisine. Even iceberg lettuce, which Western cuisines serve raw in salad, is cooked. You'll find iceberg lettuce with oyster sauce on the dinner table in many Chinese households. If you like spice, add a pinch of red pepper flakes with the ginger and salt when you're seasoning the oil.

1½ tablespoons vegetable oil

1 peeled fresh ginger slice, about the size of a quarter

Kosher salt

2 garlic cloves, thinly sliced

1 head iceberg lettuce, rinsed and spun dry, cut into 1-inch-wide pieces

2 tablespoons oyster sauce

½ teaspoon sesame oil, for garnish

1. Heat a wok over medium-high heat until a drop of water sizzles and evaporates on contact. Add the vegetable oil and swirl to coat the base of the wok. Season the oil by adding the ginger slice and a pinch of salt. Allow the ginger to sizzle in the oil for about 30 seconds, swirling gently.
2. Add the garlic and stir-fry briefly to flavor the oil, about 10 seconds. Do not let the garlic brown or burn. Add the lettuce and stir-fry until it begins to wilt slightly, 3 to 4 minutes. Drizzle the oyster sauce over the lettuce and quickly toss to coat, another 20 to 30 seconds.
3. Transfer to a platter, discard the ginger, and drizzle with the sesame oil. Serve hot.

PREP TIP: The trick here is to quickly stir-fry so the lettuce wilts but doesn't become soggy, so work quickly and keep an eye on it!

Stir-Fried Broccoli and Bamboo Shoots

SERVES 4 ; PREP TIME: 5 MINUTES ; COOK TIME: 5 MINUTES

When the "What's for dinner?" pressure mounts and you're searching for a quick and tasty vegetable side to add to the table, turn to the salad bar or produce aisle for precut broccoli florets. Keep a can of bamboo shoots in your cupboard for such an occasion. They bring crunch to this dish.

2 tablespoons vegetable oil

1 peeled fresh ginger slice, about the size of a quarter

Kosher salt

4 cups broccoli florets

2 tablespoons water

2 garlic cloves, minced

1 (8-ounce) can sliced bamboo shoots, rinsed and drained

1 tablespoon light soy sauce

1 teaspoon sesame oil

2 teaspoons toasted sesame seeds

1. Heat a wok over medium-high heat until a drop of water sizzles and evaporates on contact. Pour in the vegetable oil and swirl to coat the base of the wok. Season the oil by adding the ginger slice and a pinch of salt. Allow the ginger to sizzle in the oil for about 30 seconds, swirling gently.
2. Add the broccoli and stir-fry for 2 minutes until bright green. Add the water and cover the pan for 2 minutes to steam the broccoli.
3. Remove the cover, add the garlic, and continue stir-frying for 30 seconds. Stir in the bamboo shoots and continue to stir-fry for an additional 30 seconds.
4. Stir in the light soy and sesame oil. Remove the ginger and discard. Serve on a heated platter and garnish with sesame seeds.

VARIATION TIP: Toss in a tablespoon of Black Bean Sauce for an umami punch and add some diced tofu if you need a protein element.

Tomatoes and Eggs

SERVES 4 ; PREP TIME: 15 MINUTES ; COOK TIME: 5 MINUTES

Stir-fried Tomatoes and Eggs is one of the ultimate comfort foods for college students in China and Chinese students attending college abroad. This dish is best served in the summer, when local tomatoes are available.

2 tablespoons cooking oil

4 garlic cloves, crushed and chopped

1 tablespoon crushed and chopped ginger

4 large eggs, scrambled

2 cups fresh tomatoes, coarsely chopped

1 tablespoon brown sugar

1 tablespoon Shaoxing wine

1 tablespoon soy sauce

1 teaspoon spicy sesame oil

4 scallions, cut diagonally into ¼-inch pieces

Rice or noodles, for serving

1. In a wok, heat the cooking oil over high heat until it begins to smoke.
2. Add the garlic, ginger, and eggs to the wok and scramble until dry. Remove to a plate.
3. Add the tomatoes, sugar, wine, soy sauce, and sesame oil to the wok and stir-fry for 2 minutes.
4. Add the scrambled eggs back into the wok along with the scallions and stir-fry for 1 minute.
5. Serve immediately over rice or noodles.

VARIATION TIP: You can flavor the tomatoes with vegetable or other flavored bouillon while cooking them in the wok.

Stir-Fried Snow Peas

SERVES 4 ; PREP TIME: 5 MINUTES ; COOK TIME: 5 MINUTES

This recipe celebrates snow peas, but any vegetable at its peak would work here because clear stir-fry, the technique used in this dish, highlights the ingredient's natural flavors with ginger and salt.

2 tablespoons vegetable oil

2 peeled fresh ginger slices, each about the size of a quarter

Kosher salt

¾ pound snow peas or sugar snap peas, strings removed

1. Heat a wok over medium-high heat until a drop of water sizzles and evaporates on contact. Pour in the oil and swirl to coat the base of the wok. Season the oil by adding the ginger slices and a pinch of salt. Allow the ginger to sizzle in the oil for about 30 seconds, swirling gently.
2. Add the snow peas and, using a wok spatula, toss to coat with oil. Stir-fry for 2 to 3 minutes, until bright green and crisp tender.
3. Transfer to a platter and discard the ginger. Serve hot.

VARIATION TIP: The addition of earthy shiitake mushrooms makes this dish ultra-satisfying.

Stir-Fried Spinach with Garlic and Soy Sauce

SERVES 4 ; PREP TIME: 5 MINUTES ; COOK TIME: 5 MINUTES

For this dish, use baby spinach rather than mature spinach because you don't have to wash and chop it. The result is a superfast weeknight side dish.

1 tablespoon light soy sauce

1 teaspoon sugar

2 tablespoons vegetable oil

4 garlic cloves, thinly sliced

Kosher salt

8 ounces prewashed baby spinach

1. In a small bowl, stir together the light soy and sugar until the sugar is dissolved and set aside.
2. Heat a wok over medium-high heat until a drop of water sizzles and evaporates on contact. Pour in the oil and swirl to coat the base of the wok. Add the garlic and a pinch of salt and stir-fry, tossing until the garlic is fragrant, about 10 seconds. Using a slotted spoon, remove the garlic from the pan and set aside.
3. Add the spinach to the seasoned oil and stir-fry until the greens are just wilted and bright green. Add the sugar and soy mixture and toss to coat. Return the garlic to the wok and toss to incorporate. Transfer to a dish and serve.

PREP TIP: Make sure the spinach is spun dry in a salad spinner before adding it to the hot wok. Any extra water on the spinach leaves will make them soggy and watery in the wok.

Spicy Stir-Fried Napa Cabbage

SERVES 4 ; PREP TIME: 15 MINUTES ; COOK TIME: 10 MINUTES

Weeknights in our houses demand dishes that are tasty yet simple. This dish is both. You decide how spicy you like it by adding or subtracting chilies. For a more authentic flavor, add a pinch of ground Sichuan peppercorn.

2 tablespoons vegetable oil

3 or 4 dried chili peppers

2 peeled fresh ginger slices, each about the size of a quarter

Kosher salt

2 garlic cloves, sliced

1 head napa cabbage, shredded

1 tablespoon light soy sauce

½ tablespoon black vinegar

Freshly ground black pepper

1. Heat a wok over medium-high heat until a drop of water sizzles and evaporates on contact. Pour in the oil and swirl to coat the base of the wok. Season the oil by adding the chilies. Allow the chilies to sizzle in the oil for 15 seconds. Add the ginger slices and a pinch of salt. Allow the ginger to sizzle in the oil for about 30 seconds, swirling gently. Toss the garlic in and stir-fry briefly to flavor the oil, about 10 seconds. Do not let the garlic brown or burn.
2. Add the cabbage and stir-fry until it wilts and turns bright green, about 4 minutes. Add the light soy and black vinegar and season with a pinch each of salt and pepper. Toss to coat for another 20 to 30 seconds.
3. Transfer to a platter and discard the ginger. Serve hot.

SUBSTITUTION TIP: Don't have whole dried chilies? Use red pepper flakes instead. And hearty green savoy cabbage works great as a substitute if you can't find napa cabbage.

Dry-Fried String Beans

SERVES 4 ; PREP TIME: 10 MINUTES ; COOK TIME: 15 MINUTES

The crispy, spicy smokiness of this dish elevates green beans from boring to delicious. These green beans are essentially fried twice—once to seal in the moisture and keep them tender, and again to give them a chewy exterior. This dish is an authentic one that you can find in many Chinese restaurants.

1 tablespoon light soy sauce

1 tablespoon minced garlic

1 tablespoon doubanjiang (Chinese chili bean paste)

2 teaspoons sugar

1 teaspoon sesame oil

Kosher salt

½ cup vegetable oil

1 pound green beans, trimmed, cut in half, and blotted dry

1. In a small bowl, stir together the light soy, garlic, bean paste, sugar, sesame oil, and a pinch of salt. Set aside.
2. In a wok, heat the vegetable oil over medium-high heat to 375°F, or until it bubbles and sizzles around the end of a wooden spoon. Fry the beans in batches of a couple handfuls at a time (the beans should just cover the oil in a single layer). Gently turn the beans in the oil until they appear wrinkled, 45 seconds to 1 minute, then transfer the green beans to a paper towel–lined plate to drain.
3. Once all the beans have been cooked, carefully transfer the remaining oil to a heatproof container. Use a pair of tongs with a couple of paper towels to wipe and clean out the wok.
4. Return the wok to high heat and add 1 tablespoon of the reserved frying oil. Add the green beans and chili sauce, stir-frying until the sauce comes to a boil and coats the green beans. Transfer the beans to a platter and serve hot.

PREP TIP: Be sure to thoroughly dry the beans before frying. Moisture will prevent the beans from blistering and will spray hot oil out of the wok.

Stir-Fried Bok Choy and Mushrooms

SERVES 4 ; PREP TIME: 10 MINUTES ; COOK TIME: 10 MINUTES

You can use mature bok choy or baby bok choy in this dish. Mature bok choy has wide, thick white stems and broad dark green leaves. Baby bok choy is smaller in size, and both stems and leaves are pale green. If you can't find fresh shiitakes, white button mushrooms work well as a substitute.

3 tablespoons vegetable oil

1 peeled fresh ginger slice, about the size of a quarter

Kosher salt

½ pound fresh shiitake mushrooms, stems removed and caps cut into quarters

2 garlic cloves, minced

1½ pounds baby bok choy, sliced crosswise into 1-inch pieces

2 tablespoons Shaoxing rice wine

2 teaspoons light soy sauce

2 teaspoons sesame oil

1. Heat a wok over medium-high heat until a drop of water sizzles and evaporates on contact. Pour in the vegetable oil and swirl to coat the base of the wok. Season the oil by adding the ginger slice and a pinch of salt. Allow the ginger to sizzle in the oil for about 30 seconds, swirling gently.
2. Add the mushrooms and stir-fry for 3 to 4 minutes, until they just begin to brown. Add the garlic and stir-fry until fragrant, about 30 seconds more.
3. Add the bok choy and toss with the mushrooms. The wok may appear crowded, but the bok choy will wilt down quickly. Add the rice wine, light soy, and sesame oil. Cook for 3 to 4 minutes, tossing the vegetables constantly until they are tender.
4. Transfer the vegetables to a serving platter, discard the ginger, and serve hot.

SUBSTITUTION TIP: If the bok choy doesn't look incredibly fresh at the store, don't buy it. Wilted bok choy will turn into a watery, soggy mess if you try to stir-fry it. Use other hearty greens like kale or Swiss chard instead.

Stir-Fried Vegetable Medley

SERVES 4 TO 6 ; PREP TIME: 15 MINUTES ; COOK TIME: 15 MINUTES

You can adapt this basic vegetable stir-fry to your own liking. Cook the hardier vegetables first. All the vegetables should be cooked evenly and have a tender, yet crunchy texture. We love this medley served piping hot over a pile of steamed rice.

3 tablespoons vegetable oil

1 peeled fresh ginger slice, about the size of a quarter

Kosher salt

½ white onion, cut into 1-inch pieces

1 large carrot, peeled and cut diagonally into ¼-inch-thick slices

2 celery ribs, cut diagonally into ¼-inch-thick slices

6 fresh shiitake mushrooms, stems removed and caps thinly sliced

1 red bell pepper, cut into 1-inch pieces

1 small handful green beans, trimmed

2 garlic cloves, finely minced

2 scallions, thinly sliced

1. Heat a wok over medium-high heat until a drop of water sizzles and evaporates on contact. Pour in the oil and swirl to coat the base of the wok. Season the oil by adding the ginger slice and a pinch of salt. Let sizzle in the oil for about 30 seconds, swirling gently.
2. Add the onion, carrot, and celery to the wok and stir-fry, moving the vegetables around in the wok quickly using a spatula. When the vegetables begin to look tender, about 4 minutes, add the mushrooms and continue tossing them in the hot wok.
3. When the mushrooms look soft, add the bell pepper and continue to toss, about 4 more minutes. When the bell peppers begin to soften, add the green beans and toss until tender, about 3 more minutes. Add the garlic and toss until fragrant.
4. Transfer to a platter, discard the ginger, and garnish with the scallions. Serve hot.

VARIATION TIP: Stir in 2 to 3 tablespoons of homemade Black Bean Sauce when stir-frying the first set of vegetables.

Buddha's Delight

SERVES 4 ; PREP TIME: 20 MINUTES ; COOK TIME: 15 MINUTES

Many Buddhist monks are not only vegetarians but also avoid the five pungent vegetables: chives, garlic, scallions, leeks, and onions. Buddha is said to have avoided these smelly vegetables because they adversely affected the close quarters of communal living and also interfered with concentration and a positive meditative attitude. This dish is filled with your favorite gut-healthy vegetables, making it a perfect choice for vegetarians and Meatless Monday meals.

Small handful (about ⅓ cup) dried wood ear mushrooms

8 dried shiitake mushrooms

2 tablespoons light soy sauce

2 teaspoons sugar

1 teaspoon sesame oil

2 tablespoons vegetable oil

2 peeled fresh ginger slices, each about the size of a quarter

Kosher salt

1 delicata squash, halved, seeded, and cut into bite-size pieces

2 tablespoons Shaoxing rice wine

1 cup sugar snap peas, strings removed

1 (8-ounce) can water chestnuts, rinsed and drained

Freshly ground black pepper

1. Soak both dried mushrooms in separate bowls just covered with hot water until soft, about 20 minutes. Drain and discard the wood ear soaking liquid. Drain and save ½ cup of the shiitake liquid. To the mushroom liquid add the light soy, sugar, and sesame oil and stir to dissolve the sugar. Set aside.
2. Heat a wok over medium-high heat until a drop of water sizzles and evaporates on contact. Pour in the vegetable oil and swirl to coat the base of the wok. Season the oil by adding the ginger slices and a pinch of salt. Allow the ginger to sizzle in the oil for about 30 seconds, swirling gently.
3. Add the squash and stir-fry, tossing with the seasoned oil for about 3 minutes. Add both mushrooms and the rice wine and continue to stir-fry for 30 seconds. Add the snow peas and water chestnuts, tossing to coat with oil. Add the reserved mushroom seasoning liquid and cover. Continue cooking, stirring occasionally, until the vegetables are just tender, about 5 minutes.
4. Remove the lid and season with salt and pepper to taste. Discard the ginger and serve.

SUBSTITUTION TIP: Dried wood ear and shiitake mushrooms can be found at your local Chinese market or are available on Amazon. We like their concentrated flavor, but you could substitute fresh mushrooms of any variety.

Hunan-Style Tofu

SERVES 4 ; PREP TIME: 15 MINUTES ; COOK TIME: 10 MINUTES

The Hunan province in southern China is known for dishes that balance sweet, spicy, and salty flavors. This classic tofu dish gets its spice from bean paste and its salt from fermented black beans.

1 teaspoon cornstarch

1 tablespoon water

4 tablespoons vegetable or canola oil, divided

Kosher salt

1 pound firm tofu, drained and cut into ½-inch-thick squares, 2 inches across

3 tablespoons fermented black beans, rinsed and smashed

2 tablespoons doubanjiang (Chinese chili bean paste)

1-inch piece fresh ginger, peeled and finely minced

3 garlic cloves, finely minced

1 large red bell pepper, cut into 1-inch pieces

4 scallions, cut into 2-inch sections

1 tablespoon Shaoxing rice wine

1 teaspoon sugar

¼ cup low-sodium chicken or vegetable broth

1. In a small bowl, stir together the cornstarch and water and set aside.
2. Heat a wok over medium-high heat until a drop of water sizzles and evaporates on contact. Pour in 2 tablespoons of oil and swirl to coat the base and sides of the wok. Add a pinch of salt and arrange the tofu slices in the wok in one layer. Sear the tofu for 1 to 2 minutes, tilting the wok around to slip the oil under the tofu as it sears. When the first side is browned, using a wok spatula, carefully flip the tofu and sear for another 1 to 2 minutes until golden brown. Transfer the seared tofu to a plate and set aside.
3. Lower the heat to medium-low. Add the remaining 2 tablespoons of oil to the wok. As soon as the oil begins to slightly smoke, add the black beans, bean paste, ginger, and garlic. Stir-fry for 20 seconds, or until the oil takes on a deep red color from the bean paste.
4. Add the bell pepper and scallions and toss with the Shaoxing wine and sugar. Cook for another minute, or until the wine is nearly evaporated and the bell pepper is tender.
5. Gently fold in the fried tofu until all the ingredients in the wok are combined. Continue to cook for 45 seconds more, or until the tofu takes on a deep red color and the scallions have wilted.

6. Drizzle the chicken broth over the tofu mixture and gently stir to deglaze the wok and dissolve any of the stuck bits on the wok. Give the cornstarch-water mixture a quick stir and add to the wok. Gently stir and simmer for 2 minutes, or until the sauce becomes glossy and thick. Serve hot.

VARIATION TIP: Stir-fry 4 ounces thinly sliced pork to add to this dish to make it more traditional and heartier.

Steamed Bean Curd in a Simple Sauce

SERVES 4 ; PREP TIME: 10 MINUTES ; COOK TIME: 10 MINUTES

It's true: Tofu does not have much flavor. But when it is served with just a few delicate aromatics, its texture contributes to a beautifully composed, almost ethereal dish. If you like, you can punch this dish up with some chopped chilies or peanuts.

1 pound medium tofu

2 tablespoons light soy sauce

1 tablespoon sesame oil

2 teaspoons black vinegar

2 garlic cloves, finely minced

1 teaspoon peeled finely minced fresh ginger

½ teaspoon sugar

2 scallions, thinly sliced

1 tablespoon coarsely chopped fresh cilantro leaves

1. Remove the tofu from its packaging, taking care to keep it intact. Place it on a large plate and carefully slice it into 1- to 1½-inch-thick slices. Set aside for 5 minutes. Resting the tofu allows more of its whey to drain out.
2. Rinse a bamboo steamer basket and its lid under cold water and place it in the wok. Pour in about 2 inches of cold water, or until it comes above the bottom rim of the steamer by about ¼ to ½ inch, but not so high that the water touches the bottom of the basket.
3. Drain any extra whey from the tofu plate and place the plate in the bamboo steamer. Cover and set the wok over medium-high heat. Bring the water to a boil and steam the tofu for 6 to 8 minutes.
4. While the tofu is steaming, in a small saucepan, stir the light soy, sesame oil, vinegar, garlic, ginger, and sugar together over low heat until the sugar is dissolved.
5. Drizzle the warm sauce over the tofu and garnish with the scallions and cilantro.

PREP TIP: The water in the wok must come up high enough to submerge the bottom rim of the bamboo steamer to keep it from burning. But make sure it doesn't touch the food in the basket!

Sesame Asparagus

SERVES 4 ; PREP TIME: 5 MINUTES ; COOK TIME: 8 MINUTES

The simplest stir-fried vegetables need nothing more than a splash of soy sauce, some garlic, and a hit of aromatic sesame. For this recipe, mature asparagus works best. Select thick stalks for slicing and stir-frying. Pencil-thin asparagus are too tender and become soggy.

2 tablespoons light soy sauce

1 teaspoon sugar

1 tablespoon vegetable oil

2 large garlic cloves, coarsely chopped

2 pounds asparagus, trimmed and cut diagonally into 2-inch-long pieces

Kosher salt

2 tablespoons sesame oil

1 tablespoon toasted sesame seeds

1. In a small bowl, stir the light soy and sugar together until the sugar dissolves. Set aside.
2. Heat a wok over medium-high heat until a drop of water sizzles and evaporates on contact. Pour in the vegetable oil and swirl to coat the base of the wok. Add the garlic and stir-fry until fragrant, about 10 seconds.
3. Add the asparagus and stir-fry until crisp-tender, about 4 minutes, seasoning with a small pinch of salt while stir-frying. Add the soy sauce mixture and toss to coat the asparagus, cooking for about 1 minute more.
4. Drizzle the sesame oil over the asparagus and transfer to a serving bowl. Garnish with the sesame seeds and serve hot.

SUBSTITUTION TIP: This recipe is great for any hardy vegetable you might have on hand. If it's crunchy, it can be stir-fried. We like shredded cabbage, sliced parsnips, carrots, sugar snap peas, or green beans.

Eggplant and Tofu in Sizzling Garlic Sauce

SERVES 4 ; PREP TIME: 15 MINUTES ; COOK TIME: 15 MINUTES

The secret of this recipe is to remove the excess moisture from the eggplant to make it less bitter and prevent it from absorbing too much oil. Garnish the finished dish with a handful of chopped herbs such as cilantro and mint.

6 cups water plus 1 tablespoon, divided

1 tablespoon kosher salt

3 long Chinese eggplants (about ¾ pound), trimmed and sliced diagonally into 1-inch pieces

1½ tablespoons cornstarch, divided

1 tablespoon light soy sauce

2 teaspoons sugar

½ teaspoon dark soy sauce

3 tablespoons vegetable oil, divided

3 garlic cloves, chopped

1 teaspoon peeled minced fresh ginger

½ pound firm tofu, cut into ½-inch cubes

1. In a large bowl, combine the 6 cups of water and salt. Stir briefly to dissolve the salt and add the eggplant pieces. Place a large pot lid on top to keep the eggplant submerged in the water and let sit for 15 minutes. Drain the eggplant and pat dry with paper towels. Toss the eggplant in a bowl with a dusting of cornstarch, about 1 tablespoon.
2. In a small bowl, stir the remaining ½ tablespoon cornstarch with the remaining 1 tablespoon of water, light soy, sugar, and dark soy. Set aside.
3. Heat a wok over medium-high heat until a drop of water sizzles and evaporates on contact. Pour in 2 tablespoons of oil and swirl to coat the base of the wok and up its sides. Arrange the eggplant in a single layer in the wok.
4. Sear the eggplant on each side, about 4 minutes per side. The eggplant should be slightly charred and golden brown. Lower the heat to medium if the wok begins to smoke. Transfer the eggplant to a bowl and return the wok to the heat.
5. Add the remaining 1 tablespoon of oil and stir-fry the garlic and ginger until they are fragrant and sizzling, about 10 seconds. Add the tofu and stir-fry for 2 minutes more, then return the eggplant to the wok. Stir the sauce again and pour into the wok, tossing all the ingredients together until the sauce thickens to a dark, glossy consistency.
6. Transfer the eggplant and tofu to a platter and serve hot.

SUBSTITUTION TIP: If you can't find Chinese eggplants, conventional eggplants will purge and cook up the same way.

Beets and Tofu

SERVES 4 ; PREP TIME: 15 minutes ; COOK TIME: 5 minutes

This simple dish is a very healthy combination and makes great use of the whole beet: the root and the greens. Both are loaded with vitamins and minerals. Tofu is like vegetarian cheese. Soy milk is curdled and then filtered through cheesecloth to collect the curds, which are compressed to form tofu. Tofu is high in protein and is said to provide some protection against cancer. As a bonus, these two healthy ingredients taste great when cooked together.

2 tablespoons cooking oil

4 garlic cloves, crushed and chopped

1 tablespoon crushed and chopped ginger

1 pound extra-firm tofu, cut into 1-inch pieces

1 cup beets, stemmed and cut into ½-inch pieces

2 cups beet greens, stemmed and coarsely chopped

¼ cup hoisin sauce

4 scallions, cut diagonally into ¼-inch pieces

Rice or noodles, for serving

1. In a wok, heat the cooking oil over high heat until it begins to smoke.
2. Add the garlic, ginger, and tofu to the wok and stir-fry for 2 minutes.
3. Add the beets and stir-fry for 2 minutes.
4. Add the chopped beet greens and hoisin sauce to the wok and stir-fry for 1 additional minute.
5. Add the scallions, toss well, and serve warm over rice or noodles.

VARIATION TIP: There are other root and greens combinations that can be used in the same way as beets. Turnips and turnip greens and kohlrabi with kohlrabi greens are two other options.

Ma Po Tofu

SERVES 4 ; PREP TIME: 10 MINUTES ; COOK TIME: 20 MINUTES

This savory and spicy tofu stew is an icon in Sichuan cuisine. Served over a bowl of steamed rice, it's perfect for a cold night when you want something soothing and warming. A little piece of advice: When sautéing the peppercorns and spices, turn your hood fan on and don't breathe in too deeply—the spices can be potent! Fight the urge to stir the tofu cubes immediately upon adding them to the wok. Let them firm a bit before tossing them with the other ingredients.

½ pound ground pork

2 tablespoons Shaoxing rice wine

2 teaspoons light soy sauce

1 teaspoon peeled finely minced fresh ginger

2 teaspoons cornstarch

1½ tablespoons water

2 tablespoons vegetable oil

1 tablespoon Sichuan peppercorns, crushed

3 tablespoons doubanjiang (Chinese chili bean paste)

4 scallions, thinly sliced, divided

1 teaspoon chili oil

1 teaspoon sugar

½ teaspoon Chinese five spice powder

1 pound medium tofu, drained and cut into ½-inch cubes

1½ cups low-sodium chicken broth

Kosher salt

1 tablespoon coarsely chopped fresh cilantro leaves, for garnish

1. In a small bowl, mix together the ground pork, rice wine, light soy, and ginger. Set aside. In another small bowl, mix the cornstarch together with the water. Set aside.
2. Heat a wok over medium-high heat and pour in the vegetable oil. Add the Sichuan peppercorns and sauté gently until they begin to sizzle as the oil heats up.
3. Add the marinated pork and bean paste and stir-fry for 4 to 5 minutes, until the pork is browned and crumbled. Add half the scallions, the chili oil, sugar, and five spice powder. Continue to stir-fry for another 30 seconds, or until the scallions wilt.
4. Scatter the tofu cubes over the pork and pour in the broth. Do not stir; let the tofu cook and firm up a bit first. Cover and simmer for 15 minutes over medium heat. Uncover and stir gently. Be careful not to break up the tofu cubes too much.

5. Taste and add salt or sugar, depending on your preference. Additional sugar can calm down the spiciness if it's too hot. Stir the cornstarch and water again and add to the tofu. Gently stir until the sauce thickens.
6. Garnish with the remaining scallions and cilantro and serve hot.

SUBSTITUTION TIP: Use ground turkey instead of ground pork or make this dish vegan by using mushrooms and vegetable broth.

Chinese Broccoli (Gai Lan) with Oyster Sauce

SERVES 4 ; PREP TIME: 5 MINUTES ; COOK TIME: 5 MINUTES

Chinese broccoli, or gai lan, is broccoli's leafy green and pungent earthy cousin. Gai lan is absolutely worth a trip to an Asian specialty market, but if you don't have one near you, broccolini is a great substitute because it's a hybrid of broccoli and gai lan.

¼ cup oyster sauce

2 teaspoons light soy sauce

1 teaspoon sesame oil

2 tablespoons vegetable oil

4 peeled fresh ginger slices, each about the size of a quarter

4 garlic cloves, peeled

Kosher salt

2 bunches Chinese broccoli or broccolini, tough ends trimmed

2 tablespoons water

1. In a small bowl, stir together the oyster sauce, light soy, and sesame oil and set aside.
2. Heat a wok over medium-high heat until a drop of water sizzles and evaporates on contact. Pour in the vegetable oil and swirl to coat the base of the wok. Add the ginger, garlic, and a pinch of salt. Allow the aromatics to sizzle in the oil, swirling gently for about 10 seconds.
3. Add the broccoli and stir, tossing until coated with oil and bright green. Add the water and cover to steam the broccoli for about 3 minutes, or until the stalks can easily be pierced with a knife. Remove the ginger and garlic and discard.
4. Stir in the sauce and toss to coat until hot. Transfer to a serving plate.

VARIATION TIP: Call us crazy, but this recipe is delicious with small, salty, smoked oysters tossed in. It's not authentic, but it is similar to another traditional dish that utilizes shredded, dried scallops (which are hard to find and very expensive).

FISH AND SHELLFISH

Drunken Shrimp

SERVES 4 ; PREP TIME: 30 MINUTES ; COOK TIME: 10 MINUTES

This recipe highlights the ingenuity of Chinese cooking by repurposing the marinade as the finishing liquid. The trick is not to marinate the shrimp for more than 30 minutes. Shrimp are so delicate they can become tough if they sit too long in the marinade. Goji berries add a sweet-tart flavor to this dish, but they are optional, or you can substitute finely chopped dried cranberries.

2 cups Shaoxing rice wine

4 peeled fresh ginger slices, each about the size of a quarter

2 tablespoons dried goji berries (optional)

2 teaspoons sugar

1 pound jumbo shrimp (U21–25), peeled and deveined, tails left on

2 tablespoons vegetable oil

Kosher salt

2 teaspoons cornstarch

1. In a wide mixing bowl, stir together the rice wine, ginger, goji berries (if using), and sugar until the sugar is dissolved. Add the shrimp and cover. Marinate in the refrigerator for 20 to 30 minutes.
2. Pour the shrimp and marinade into a colander set over a bowl. Reserve ½ cup of the marinade and discard the rest.
3. Heat a wok over medium-high heat until a drop of water sizzles and evaporates on contact. Pour in the oil and swirl to coat the base of the wok. Season the oil by adding a small pinch of salt, and swirl gently.
4. Add the shrimp and vigorously stir-fry, adding a pinch of salt as you flip and toss the shrimp around in the wok. Keep moving the shrimp around for about 3 minutes, until they just turn pink.
5. Stir the cornstarch into the reserved marinade and pour it over the shrimp. Toss the shrimp and coat with the marinade. It will thicken into a glossy sauce as it begins to boil, about another 5 minutes more.
6. Transfer the shrimp and goji berries to a platter, discard the ginger, and serve hot.

Shanghainese-Style Stir-Fried Shrimp

SERVES 4 ; PREP TIME: 5 MINUTES ; COOK TIME: 10 MINUTES

Terri's mother, Alice, often cooks this as a side dish, but it would be terrific over steamed rice and some simple stir-fried vegetables. Leftovers are also fantastic chopped up and added to fried rice!

1 pound medium-large shrimp (U31–40), peeled and deveined, tails left on

2 tablespoons vegetable oil

Kosher salt

2 teaspoons Shaoxing rice wine

2 scallions, finely julienned

1. Using sharp kitchen scissors or a paring knife, slice the shrimp in half lengthwise, keeping the tail section intact. As the shrimp is stir-fried, cutting it this way will give more surface area and create a unique shape and texture!
2. Blot the shrimp dry with paper towels and keep dry. The drier the shrimp, the more flavorful the dish. You can keep the shrimp refrigerated, rolled up in a paper towel, for up to 2 hours before cooking.
3. Heat a wok over medium-high heat until a drop of water sizzles and evaporates on contact. Pour in the oil and swirl to coat the base of the wok. Season the oil by adding a small pinch of salt, and swirl gently.
4. Add the shrimp all at once to the hot wok. Toss and flip quickly for 2 to 3 minutes, until the shrimp just begins to turn pink. Season with another small pinch of salt, and add the rice wine. Let the wine boil off while you continue stir-frying, about another 2 minutes. The shrimp should separate and curl, still attached at the tail.
5. Transfer to a serving platter and garnish with the scallions. Serve hot.

VARIATION TIP: Mom loves to add tomatoes to this dish to make it richer and sweeter. Just as the shrimp turns pink, remove it from the wok and toss in 2 to 3 chopped Roma tomatoes. Stir-fry the tomatoes until they begin to break down, then season with a small pinch of salt and sugar. Toss in the shrimp and continue cooking.

Sweet-and-Sour Shrimp

SERVES 4 ; PREP TIME: 20 MINUTES ; COOK TIME: 5 MINUTES

Chinese sweet-and-sour sauce was created in China in the 18th century. It was originally used as a dipping sauce and eventually came to be used as a finishing sauce for stir-fries. The iconic combination of sweet and sour can be created with a variety of ingredients. The sour can come from vinegar, lemon, or limes, for example, while the sweet can come from sugar, honey, or fruit juices.

1 pound medium shrimp, peeled, deveined, and cut in half lengthwise

¼ cup plus 2 tablespoons cornstarch, divided

¼ cup cooking oil

1 tablespoon crushed and chopped ginger

2 garlic cloves, crushed and chopped

1 medium bell pepper, cut into 1-inch pieces

1 (8-ounce) can pineapple chunks, with juice reserved

¼ cup rice vinegar

2 tablespoons ketchup

4 scallions, cut into 1-inch pieces

Rice or noodles, for serving

1. Toss the shrimp with ¼ cup cornstarch in a plastic bag or a covered medium bowl.
2. Heat the cooking oil, ginger, and garlic in a wok over high heat until the garlic is lightly browned.
3. Add the shrimp and shallow fry for 2 to 3 minutes, until it is lightly browned.
4. Remove the shrimp from the wok and set aside.
5. Remove and discard all but 2 tablespoons oil from the wok.
6. Add the pepper and pineapple and stir-fry for 1 minute.
7. Add the vinegar, ketchup, pineapple juice, and the remaining 2 tablespoons cornstarch to the wok and cook, stirring, until a glaze forms.
8. Return the shrimp to the wok and garnish with the scallions. Serve with steamed rice or noodles.

Salt and Pepper Shrimp

SERVES 4 ; PREP TIME: 20 MINUTES ; COOK TIME: 10 MINUTES

This recipe for deep-fried crispy shrimp with a little bit of heat and salt draws inspiration from the signature salt and pepper crab dish at San Francisco Chinatown's beloved R&G Lounge. Dry the shrimp thoroughly before frying, because moisture will make the cornstarch gummy, preventing the shrimp from crisping.

1 tablespoon kosher salt

1½ teaspoons Sichuan peppercorns

1½ pounds large shrimp (U31–35), peeled and deveined, tails left on

½ cup vegetable oil

1 cup cornstarch

4 scallions, sliced diagonally

1 jalapeño pepper, halved and seeded, thinly sliced

6 garlic cloves, thinly sliced

1. In a small sauté pan or skillet over medium heat, toast the salt and peppercorns until aromatic, shaking and stirring frequently to avoid burning. Transfer to a bowl to cool completely. Grind the salt and peppercorns together in a spice grinder or with a mortar and pestle. Transfer to a bowl and set aside.
2. Blot the shrimp dry with a paper towel.
3. In a wok, heat the oil over medium-high heat to 375°F, or until it bubbles and sizzles around the end of a wooden spoon.
4. Put the cornstarch in a large bowl. Just before you are ready to fry the shrimp, toss half the shrimp to coat in the cornstarch and shake off any excess cornstarch.
5. Fry the shrimp for 1 to 2 minutes, until they turn pink. Using a wok skimmer, transfer the fried shrimp to a rack set over a baking sheet to drain. Repeat the process with the remaining shrimp of tossing in cornstarch, frying, and transferring to the rack to drain.
6. Once all of the shrimp have been cooked, carefully remove all but 2 tablespoons of the oil and return the wok to medium heat. Add the scallions, jalapeño, and garlic and stir-fry until the scallions and jalapeño turn bright green and the garlic is aromatic. Return the shrimp to the wok, season to taste with the salt and pepper mixture (you may not use it all), and toss to coat. Transfer the shrimp to a platter and serve hot.

PREP TIP: Don't have a spice grinder or mortar and pestle? Put the salt and peppercorns in a small (unbreakable) bowl, and use the end of a wooden spoon to grind the spices.

Scallops with Bacon, Napa Cabbage, and Oyster Sauce

SERVES 4 ; PREP TIME: 20 MINUTES ; COOK TIME: 5 MINUTES

This super quick, Cantonese-style stir-fry takes advantage of the sweet, cured flavor and fat from the bacon to keep the scallops moist and tender. The flavor base of ginger, garlic, and scallions blends nicely with the salty umami of the fermented oyster sauce. For a smoky flavor, use hickory- or maple-smoked bacon.

¼ pound thick-sliced bacon (2 or 3 slices), cut into ½-inch pieces

4 garlic cloves, crushed and chopped

1 tablespoon crushed and chopped ginger

½ pound fresh sea scallops, cut in half

2 cups Napa cabbage, cut diagonally into 1-inch pieces

2 tablespoons oyster sauce

4 scallions, cut diagonally into ¼-inch pieces

Rice or noodles, for serving

1. In a wok, stir-fry the bacon, garlic, and ginger for 2 minutes, or until bacon is lightly browned.
2. Add the scallops and stir-fry for 1 minute.
3. Add the cabbage to the mixture and stir-fry for 1 minute.
4. Add the oyster sauce and scallions, toss until well combined, and serve over rice or noodles.

INGREDIENT TIP: Fresh, dry sea scallops are the best choice if you can get them, as they sear more easily. If you get frozen, you can thaw them overnight in their bag. If time is short, you can thaw them by submerging the bag in warm tap water.

Walnut Shrimp

SERVES 4 ; PREP TIME: 15 MINUTES ; COOK TIME: 25 MINUTES

Celebratory Chinese banquets can be composed of 12 courses, of which walnut shrimp are usually the fourth. The toasty, crunchy sweet walnuts pair beautifully with the shrimp. The tangy creamy sauce pulls it all together.

Nonstick vegetable oil spray

1 pound jumbo shrimp (U21–25), peeled

25 to 30 walnut halves

3 cups vegetable oil, for frying

2 tablespoons sugar

2 tablespoons water

¼ cup mayonnaise

3 tablespoons sweetened condensed milk

¼ teaspoon rice vinegar

Kosher salt

⅓ cup cornstarch

1. Line a baking sheet with parchment paper and lightly spray with cooking spray. Set aside.
2. Butterfly the shrimp by holding it on a cutting board curved-side down. Starting from the head area, insert the tip of a paring knife three-quarters of the way into the shrimp. Make a slice down the center of the shrimp's back to the tail. Don't cut all the way through the shrimp, and do not cut into the tail area. Open the shrimp like a book and spread it flat. Wipe away the vein (the shrimp's digestive tract) if it is visible and rinse the shrimp under cold water, then blot dry with a paper towel. Set aside.
3. In a wok, heat the oil over medium-high heat to 375°F, or until it bubbles and sizzles around the end of a wooden spoon. Fry the walnuts until golden brown, 3 to 4 minutes, and, using a wok skimmer, transfer the walnuts to a paper towel–lined plate. Set aside and turn off the heat.
4. In a small saucepan, stir together the sugar and water and bring to a boil over medium-high heat, stirring occasionally, until the sugar dissolves. Lower the heat to medium and simmer to reduce the syrup for 5 minutes, or until the syrup is thick and glossy. Add the walnuts and toss to completely coat them with the syrup. Transfer the nuts to the prepared baking sheet and set aside to cool. The sugar should harden around the nuts and form a candied shell.
5. In a small bowl, stir together the mayonnaise, condensed milk, rice vinegar, and a pinch of salt. Set aside.

6. Bring the wok oil back to 375°F over medium-high heat. As the oil is heating, season the shrimp lightly with a pinch of salt. In a mixing bowl, toss the shrimp with the cornstarch until well coated. Working in small batches, shake the excess cornstarch off the shrimp and fry in the oil, moving them quickly in the oil so they don't stick together. Fry the shrimp for 2 to 3 minutes until golden brown.
7. Transfer to a clean mixing bowl and drizzle the sauce over. Gently fold until the shrimp are evenly coated. Arrange the shrimp on a platter and garnish with the candied walnuts. Serve hot.

PREP TIP: Butterflying the shrimp isn't necessary, but it flattens the shrimp so that it cooks up faster, looks bigger, and gives you more shrimp-to-sauce ratio. It takes a few extra moments to butterfly the shrimp, but it's totally worth it.

Velveted Scallops

SERVES 4 ; PREP TIME: 35 MINUTES ; COOK TIME: 5 MINUTES

Velveting is an indispensable Chinese cooking technique used to tenderize seafood, poultry, and meat. It's the secret to keeping these ingredients from drying out and becoming tough while stir-frying. Here the scallops are velveted, quickly blanched, and then stir-fried until just heated through. This method allows the delicate sweet sea flavor of the scallops to shine through.

1 large egg white

2 tablespoons cornstarch

2 tablespoons Shaoxing rice wine, divided

1 teaspoon kosher salt, divided

1 pound fresh sea scallops, rinsed, muscle removed, and patted dry

3 tablespoons vegetable oil, divided

1 tablespoon light soy sauce

¼ cup freshly squeezed orange juice

Grated zest of 1 orange

Red pepper flakes (optional)

2 scallions, green part only, thinly sliced, for garnish

1. In a large bowl, combine the egg white, cornstarch, 1 tablespoon of rice wine, and ½ teaspoon of salt and stir with a small whisk until the cornstarch completely dissolves and is no longer lumpy. Toss in the scallops and refrigerate for 30 minutes.
2. Remove the scallops from the fridge. Bring a medium-size pot of water to boil. Add 1 tablespoon of vegetable oil and reduce to a simmer. Add the scallops to the simmering water and cook for 15 to 20 seconds, stirring continuously until the scallops just turn opaque (the scallops will not be completely cooked through). Using a wok skimmer, transfer the scallops to a paper towel–lined baking sheet and pat dry with paper towels.
3. In a glass measuring cup, combine the remaining 1 tablespoon of rice wine, light soy, orange juice, orange zest, and a pinch of red pepper flakes (if using) and set aside.
4. Heat a wok over medium-high heat until a drop of water sizzles and evaporates on contact. Pour in the remaining 2 tablespoons of oil and swirl to coat the base of the wok. Season the oil by adding the remaining ½ teaspoon salt.
5. Add the velveted scallops to the wok and swirl in the sauce. Stir-fry the scallops until they are just cooked through, about 1 minute. Transfer to a serving dish and garnish with the scallions.

INGREDIENT TIP: The muscle or "foot," a little dense piece that attaches the scallop to its shell, is typically removed in the United States because it is thought to be bland and a little tough. It's up to you to remove or not remove. Need some help identifying the foot? Ask your fishmonger for help.

Stir-Fried Fish with Ginger and Bok Choy

SERVES 4 ; PREP TIME: 15 MINUTES ; COOK TIME: 15 MINUTES

Marinating fish in a slurry of egg white, cornstarch, and rice wine prior to cooking will result in a tender and flavorful fillet. Any protein and vegetable combination will work with this recipe. Shrimp with asparagus is a favorite of ours.

1 large egg white

1 tablespoon Shaoxing rice wine

2 teaspoons cornstarch

1 teaspoon sesame oil

½ teaspoon light soy sauce

1 pound boneless fish fillets, cut into 2-inch chunks

4 tablespoons vegetable oil, divided

Kosher salt

4 peeled fresh ginger slices, about the size of a quarter

3 heads baby bok choy, cut into bite-size pieces

1 garlic clove, minced

1. In a medium bowl, mix together the egg white, rice wine, cornstarch, sesame oil, and light soy. Add the fish to the marinade, and stir to coat. Marinate for 10 minutes.
2. Heat a wok over medium-high heat until a drop of water sizzles and evaporates on contact. Pour in 2 tablespoons of vegetable oil and swirl to coat the base of the wok. Season the oil by adding a small pinch of salt, and swirl gently.
3. With a slotted spoon, lift the fish from the marinade and sear in the wok for about 2 minutes on each side, until lightly browned on both sides. Transfer the fish to a plate and set aside.
4. Add the remaining 2 tablespoons of vegetable oil to the wok. Add another pinch of salt and the ginger and season the oil, swirling gently for 30 seconds. Add the bok choy and garlic and stir-fry for 3 to 4 minutes, tossing constantly, until the bok choy is tender.
5. Return the fish to the wok and gently toss together with the bok choy until combined. Season lightly with another pinch of salt. Transfer to a platter, discard the ginger, and serve immediately.

Mussels in Black Bean Sauce

SERVES 4 ; PREP TIME: 10 MINUTES ; COOK TIME: 10 MINUTES

These delicious mussels pair beautifully with the salty-savory black bean sauce and Shaoxing rice wine, especially when served over heaps of steamed jasmine rice. If you can't find PEI mussels, clams or other mussels will work just as well.

3 tablespoons vegetable oil

2 peeled fresh ginger slices, each about the size of a quarter

Kosher salt

2 scallions, cut into 2-inch-long pieces

4 large garlic cloves, thinly sliced

2 pounds live PEI mussels, scrubbed and debearded

2 tablespoons Shaoxing rice wine

2 tablespoons Black Bean Sauce or store-bought black bean sauce

2 teaspoons sesame oil

½ bunch fresh cilantro, coarsely chopped

1. Heat a wok over medium-high heat until a drop of water sizzles and evaporates on contact. Pour in the vegetable oil and swirl to coat the base of the wok. Season the oil by adding the ginger slices and a small pinch of salt. Allow the ginger to sizzle in the oil for about 30 seconds, swirling gently.
2. Toss in the scallions and garlic and stir-fry for 10 seconds, or until the scallions are wilted.
3. Add the mussels and toss to coat with the oil. Pour the rice wine down the sides of the wok and toss briefly. Cover and steam for 6 to 8 minutes, until the mussels are opened.
4. Uncover and add the black bean sauce, tossing to coat the mussels. Cover and let steam for another 2 minutes. Uncover and pick through, removing any mussels that have not opened.
5. Drizzle the mussels with the sesame oil. Toss briefly until the sesame oil is fragrant. Discard the ginger, transfer the mussels to a platter, and garnish with the cilantro.

Coconut Curry Crab

SERVES 4 ; PREP TIME: 10 MINUTES ; COOK TIME: 15 MINUTES

Crabmeat simmered in a luscious coconut curry comes together in just minutes. It's wonderful if you have access to cracked fresh crab for this recipe, but we love this recipe as a way to cook from our pantry and use canned crab more often than not.

2 tablespoons vegetable oil

2 peeled slices fresh ginger, about the size of a quarter

Kosher salt

1 shallot, thinly sliced

1 tablespoon curry powder

1 (13.5-ounce) can coconut milk

¼ teaspoon sugar

1 tablespoon Shaoxing rice wine

1 pound canned crabmeat, drained and picked through to remove shell pieces

Freshly ground black pepper

¼ cup chopped fresh cilantro or flat-leaf parsley, for garnish

Cooked rice, for serving

1. Heat a wok over medium-high heat until a drop of water sizzles and evaporates on contact. Pour in the oil and swirl to coat the base of the wok. Season the oil by adding the ginger slices and a pinch of salt. Allow the ginger to sizzle in the oil for about 30 seconds, swirling gently.
2. Add the shallot and stir-fry for about 10 seconds. Add the curry powder and stir until fragrant for another 10 seconds.
3. Stir in the coconut milk, sugar, and rice wine, cover the wok, and cook for 5 minutes.
4. Stir in the crab, cover with the lid, and cook until heated through, about 5 minutes. Remove the lid, adjust the seasoning with salt and pepper, and discard the ginger. Ladle over the top of a bowl of rice and garnish with chopped cilantro.

SUBSTITUTION TIP: You can use shrimp instead of crab and toss it all together with rice noodles.

Deep-Fried Black Pepper Squid

SERVES 4 ; PREP TIME: 10 MINUTES ; COOK TIME: 10 MINUTES

Forget the fried calamari you normally order at your favorite Italian places for appetizers. These tender squid pieces are lightly battered and fried and have just enough heat from the black pepper to keep you from needing any dipping sauces. To punch things up a bit, you can also batter and fry thin slices of jalapeño peppers.

3 cups vegetable oil

1 pound squid tubes and tentacles, cleaned and tubes cut into ⅓-inch rings

½ cup rice flour

Kosher salt

¼ teaspoon freshly ground black pepper

¾ cup sparkling water, kept ice cold

2 tablespoons coarsely chopped fresh cilantro

1. Pour the oil into the wok; the oil should be about 1 to 1½ inches deep. Bring the oil to 375°F over medium-high heat. You can tell the oil is at the right temperature when the oil bubbles and sizzles around the end of a wooden spoon when it is dipped in. Blot the squid dry with paper towels.
2. Meanwhile, in a shallow bowl, stir the rice flour with a pinch of salt and the pepper. Whisk in just enough sparkling water to form a thin batter. Fold in the squid and, working in batches, lift up the squid from the batter using a wok skimmer or slotted spoon, shaking off any excess. Carefully lower into the hot oil.
3. Cook the squid for about 3 minutes, until golden brown and crisp. Using a wok skimmer, remove the calamari from the oil and transfer to a paper towel–lined plate and season lightly with salt. Repeat with the remaining squid.
4. Transfer the squid to a platter and garnish with the cilantro. Serve hot.

SUBSTITUTION TIP: You can fry small bay scallops or shrimp in this manner as well; just make sure to blot the seafood with paper towels to remove as much surface moisture as possible before frying.

Seafood and Veggie Stir-Fry with Crispy Rice Noodles

SERVES 4 ; PREP TIME: 15 MINUTES ; COOK TIME: 15 MINUTES

This dish shows you how to achieve the white crispy noodles that garnish many stir-fries in Chinese restaurants. Use the thinnest dried vermicelli rice noodles or dried bean thread noodles—they look very similar in the package. Fried in oil, they puff up, giving any dish a satisfying crunch.

1 cup vegetable oil, divided

3 peeled fresh ginger slices, each about the size of a quarter

Kosher salt

1 red bell pepper, cut into 1-inch pieces

1 small white onion, sliced into thin, long vertical strips

1 large handful snow peas, strings removed

2 large garlic cloves, finely minced

½ pound shrimp (any size, peeled and deveined) or fish, cut into 1-inch pieces

1 tablespoon Black Bean Sauce or store-bought black bean sauce (optional)

½ pound dried vermicelli rice noodles or bean thread noodles

1. Heat a wok over medium-high heat until a drop of water sizzles and evaporates on contact. Pour in 2 tablespoons of oil and swirl to coat the base of the wok. Season the oil by adding the ginger slices and a small pinch of salt. Allow the ginger to sizzle in the oil for about 30 seconds, swirling gently.
2. Add the bell pepper and onion and stir-fry quickly by tossing and flipping them around in the wok using a wok spatula. Season lightly with salt and continue to stir-fry for 4 to 6 minutes, until the onion looks soft and translucent. Add the snow peas and garlic, tossing and flipping until the garlic is fragrant, about another minute. Transfer the vegetables to a plate.
3. Heat another 1 tablespoon of oil and add the shrimp or fish. Gently toss and season lightly with a small pinch of salt. Stir-fry for 3 to 4 minutes, or until the shrimp turn pink or the fish begins to flake. Return the vegetables and toss everything together for 1 minute more. Discard the ginger and transfer the shrimp to a platter. Tent with foil to keep warm.
4. Wipe out the wok and return to medium-high heat. Pour in the remaining oil (about ¾ cup) and heat to 375°F, or until it bubbles and sizzles around the end of a wooden spoon. As soon as the oil is at temperature, add the dried noodles. They will immediately begin to puff and rise from the oil. Using tongs, flip the cloud of noodles

over if you need to fry the top, and carefully lift from the oil and transfer to a paper towel–lined plate to drain and cool.

5. Gently break the noodles into smaller chunks and scatter over the stir-fried vegetables and shrimp. Serve immediately.

SUBSTITUTION TIP: Change up the seafood and use scallops to elevate this dish into a showstopper.

Whole Steamed Fish with Sizzling Ginger and Scallions

SERVES 4 ; PREP TIME: 10 MINUTES ; COOK TIME: 20 MINUTES

We like to steam virtually any whitefish whole—sea bass, red snapper, yellowtail snapper, rockfish, trout, or halibut. We have also steamed whole salmon this way with great success. When buying a whole fish from the market, ask the fishmonger to clean it for you so it's ready to go as soon as you get it home. For a little spice, add slivers of thinly sliced fresh chilies to the sauce.

FOR THE FISH

1 whole whitefish, about 2 pounds, head on and cleaned

½ cup kosher salt, for cleaning

3 scallions, sliced into 3-inch pieces

4 peeled fresh ginger slices, each about the size of a quarter

2 tablespoons Shaoxing rice wine

FOR THE SAUCE

2 tablespoons light soy sauce

1 tablespoon sesame oil

2 teaspoons sugar

FOR THE SIZZLING GINGER OIL

3 tablespoons vegetable oil

2 tablespoons peeled fresh ginger finely julienned into thin strips

2 scallions, thinly sliced

Red onion, thinly sliced (optional)

Cilantro (optional)

TO MAKE THE FISH

1. Rub the fish inside and out with the kosher salt. Rinse the fish and pat dry with paper towels.
2. On a plate large enough to fit into a bamboo steamer basket, make a bed using half of each of the scallions and ginger. Lay the fish on top and stuff the remaining scallions and ginger inside the fish. Pour the rice wine over the fish.
3. Rinse a bamboo steamer basket and its lid under cold water and place it in the wok. Pour in about 2 inches of cold water, or until it comes above the bottom rim of the steamer by about ¼ to ½ inch, but not so high that the water touches the bottom of the basket. Bring the water to a boil.

4. Place the plate in the steamer basket and cover. Steam the fish over medium heat for 15 minutes (add 2 minutes for every half pound more). Before removing from the wok, poke the fish with a fork near the head. If the flesh flakes, it's done. If the flesh still sticks together, steam for 2 minutes more.

TO MAKE THE SAUCE

5. While the fish is steaming, in a small pan, warm the light soy, sesame oil, and sugar over low heat, and set aside.
6. Once the fish is cooked, transfer to a clean platter. Discard the cooking liquid and aromatics from the steaming plate. Pour the warm soy sauce mixture over the fish. Tent with foil to keep it warm while you prepare the oil.

TO MAKE THE SIZZLING GINGER OIL

7. In a small saucepan, heat the vegetable oil over medium heat. Just before it starts to smoke, add half of each of the ginger and scallions and fry for 10 seconds. Pour the hot sizzling oil over the top of the fish. Garnish with the remaining ginger and scallions and serve immediately.

SUBSTITUTION TIP: Although any whole, white flaky fish works well with this preparation, we've even had success steaming clams and mussels in this manner. The sizzling ginger oil is fantastic with the shellfish.

Deep-Fried Oysters with Chili-Garlic Confetti

SERVES 4 ; PREP TIME: 15 MINUTES ; COOK TIME: 15 MINUTES

Deep-fried oysters are a common item found on banquet tables during Lunar New Year celebrations. These are easy to fry up and enjoy at home, and the fried confetti garnish is colorful and gives the whole dish a zippy heat. In fact, fry up the confetti garnish and use it on vegetables, pork chops, fish, or anything you want.

1 (16-ounce) container small shucked oysters

½ cup rice flour

½ cup all-purpose flour, divided

½ teaspoon baking powder

Kosher salt

Ground white pepper

¼ teaspoon onion powder

¾ cup sparkling water, chilled

1 teaspoon sesame oil

3 cups vegetable oil

3 large garlic cloves, thinly sliced

1 small red chili, finely diced

1 small green chili, finely diced

1 scallion, thinly sliced

1. Drain the shucked oysters in a colander for 10 minutes to remove as much extra liquid as possible.
2. In a mixing bowl, stir together the rice flour, ¼ cup of all-purpose flour, baking powder, a pinch each of salt and white pepper, and onion powder. Add the sparkling water and sesame oil, mix until smooth, and set aside.
3. In a wok, heat the vegetable oil over medium-high heat to 375°F, or until it bubbles and sizzles around the end of a wooden spoon.
4. Blot the oysters with a paper towel and dredge in the remaining ¼ cup of all-purpose flour. Dip the oysters one at a time in the rice flour batter and carefully lower into the hot oil.
5. Fry the oysters for 3 to 4 minutes, or until golden brown. Transfer to a wire cooling rack fitted over a baking sheet to drain. Sprinkle lightly with salt.
6. Return the oil temperature to 375°F and fry the garlic and chilies briefly until they are crispy but still brightly colored, about 45 seconds. With a wire skimmer, lift out of the oil and place on a paper towel–lined plate.

7. Arrange the oysters on a platter and sprinkle the garlic and chilies over. Garnish with the sliced scallions and serve immediately.

PREP TIP: Make sure the sparkling water is ice cold for a light, crispy coating. We like to use a combination of rice flour and all-purpose flour. The rice flour keeps the batter from becoming dense and soggy.

POULTRY AND EGGS

Tangerine Zest Chicken

SERVES 4 ; PREP TIME: 15 MINUTES ; COOK TIME: 20 MINUTES

Make this when you're deep into the winter months, craving something sunny and bright. Tangerines hit peak season around the same time as the Lunar New Year. There is the extra step to fry the chicken to crispy, tasty nuggets before tossing them in the spicy-tangy sauce, but it's worth it. You'll wonder why you ever ordered takeout.

3 large egg whites

2 tablespoons cornstarch

1½ tablespoons light soy sauce, divided

¼ teaspoon ground white pepper

¾ pound boneless, skinless chicken thighs, cut into bite-size pieces

3 cups vegetable oil

4 peeled fresh ginger slices, each about the size of a quarter

1 teaspoon Sichuan peppercorns, slightly cracked

Kosher salt

½ yellow onion, thinly sliced into ¼-inch-wide strips

Peel of 1 tangerine, shredded into ⅛-inch-thick strips

Juice of 2 tangerines (about ½ cup)

2 teaspoons sesame oil

½ teaspoon rice vinegar

Light brown sugar

2 scallions, thinly sliced, for garnish

1 tablespoon sesame seeds, for garnish

1. In a mixing bowl, using a fork or whisk, beat the egg whites until frothy and until the tighter clumps are foamy. Stir in the cornstarch, 2 teaspoons of light soy, and white pepper until well blended. Fold in the chicken and marinate for 10 minutes.
2. Pour the oil into the wok; the oil should be about 1 to 1½ inches deep. Bring the oil to 375°F over medium-high heat. You can tell the oil is at the right temperature when you dip the end of a wooden spoon into the oil. If the oil bubbles and sizzles around it, the oil is ready.
3. Using a slotted spoon or wok skimmer, lift the chicken from the marinade and shake off the excess. Carefully lower into the hot oil. Fry the chicken in batches for 3 to 4 minutes, or until the chicken is golden brown and crispy on the surface. Transfer to a paper towel–lined plate.
4. Pour out all but 1 tablespoon of oil from the wok and set it over medium-high heat. Swirl the oil to coat the base of the wok. Season the oil by adding the ginger, peppercorns,

and a pinch of salt. Allow the ginger and peppercorns to sizzle in the oil for about 30 seconds, swirling gently.

5. Add the onion and stir-fry, tossing and flipping with a wok spatula for 2 to 3 minutes, or until the onion becomes soft and translucent. Add the tangerine peel and stir-fry for another minute, or until fragrant.
6. Add the tangerine juice, sesame oil, vinegar, and a pinch of brown sugar. Bring the sauce to a boil and simmer for about 6 minutes, until reduced by half. It should be syrupy and very tangy. Taste and add a pinch of salt, if needed.
7. Turn off the heat and add the fried chicken, tossing to coat with the sauce. Transfer the chicken to a platter, discard the ginger, and garnish with the sliced scallions and sesame seeds. Serve hot.

SUBSTITUTION TIP: We know what you're thinking: Why isn't there a recipe for orange chicken in this cookbook? Well, this is it. You can substitute orange zest and juice, for sure. If you don't have Sichuan peppercorns, add a pinch of red pepper flakes instead.

Cashew Chicken

SERVES 4 TO 6 ; PREP TIME: 20 MINUTES ; COOK TIME: 10 MINUTES

In George Selden's children's book *The Cricket in Times Square*, Mario enjoys a meal in Chinatown while shopping for a cage and mulberry leaves for his pet cricket, Chester. One of the dishes was most likely cashew chicken, and as a young girl obsessed with food, Terri started to recreate the dish from just the descriptions in the book. Many iterations later, here is a fresh and tasty version to make at home.

1 tablespoon light soy sauce

2 teaspoons Shaoxing rice wine

2 teaspoons cornstarch

1 teaspoon sesame oil

½ teaspoon ground Sichuan peppercorns

¾ pound boneless, skinless, chicken thighs, cut into 1-inch cubes

2 tablespoons vegetable oil

½-inch piece peeled finely minced fresh ginger

Kosher salt

½ red bell pepper, cut into ½-inch pieces

1 small zucchini, cut into ½-inch pieces

2 garlic cloves, minced

½ cup unsalted dry roasted cashews

2 scallions, white and green parts separated, thinly sliced

1. In a medium bowl, stir together the light soy, rice wine, cornstarch, sesame oil, and Sichuan pepper. Add the chicken and stir gently to coat. Let it marinate for 15 minutes, or for enough time to prepare the rest of the ingredients.
2. Heat a wok over medium-high heat until a drop of water sizzles and evaporates on contact. Pour in the vegetable oil and swirl to coat the base of the wok. Season the oil by adding the ginger and a pinch of salt. Allow the ginger to sizzle in the oil for about 30 seconds, swirling gently.
3. Using tongs, lift the chicken from the marinade and transfer to the wok, reserving the marinade. Stir-fry the chicken for 4 to 5 minutes, until no longer pink. Add the red bell pepper, zucchini, and garlic and stir-fry for 2 to 3 minutes, or until the vegetables are tender.
4. Pour in the marinade and mix to coat the other ingredients. Bring the marinade to a boil and continue to stir-fry for 1 to 2 minutes, until the sauce turns thick and glossy. Stir in the cashews and cook for another minute.
5. Transfer to a serving plate, garnish with the scallions, and serve hot.

PREP TIP: You can marinate the chicken longer, overnight or during your workday. Just leave out half the soy sauce and add it during the cooking process instead.

Kung Pao Chicken

SERVES 4 TO 6 ; PREP TIME: 20 MINUTES ; COOK TIME: 10 MINUTES

As a young child, Terri thought kung pao chicken was onomatopoeia for the sensation of the spicy chicken as it hit her taste buds (kung–POW!). In reality, the dish hails from China's Sichuan province, famous for mouth-numbing Sichuan peppercorns and fiery chilies. Serve this with lots of steamed rice to help tame the heat from the chilies.

3 teaspoons light soy sauce

2½ teaspoons cornstarch

2 teaspoons Chinese black vinegar

1 teaspoon Shaoxing rice wine

1 teaspoon sesame oil

¾ pound boneless, skinless, chicken thighs, cut into 1-inch cubes

2 tablespoons vegetable oil

6 to 8 whole dried red chilies, or 1 teaspoon red pepper flakes

3 scallions, white and green parts separated, thinly sliced

2 garlic cloves, minced

1 teaspoon peeled minced fresh ginger

¼ cup unsalted dry roasted peanuts

1. In a medium bowl, stir together the light soy, cornstarch, black vinegar, rice wine, and sesame oil until the cornstarch is dissolved. Add the chicken and stir gently to coat. Marinate for 10 to 15 minutes, or enough time to prepare the rest of the ingredients.
2. Heat a wok over medium-high heat until a drop of water sizzles and evaporates on contact. Pour in the vegetable oil and swirl to coat the base of the wok.
3. Add the chilies and stir-fry for about 10 seconds, or until they have just begun to blacken and the oil is slightly fragrant. (Note: Turn on your stove's exhaust fan, because stir-frying dried chilies on high heat can get a little smoky.) Add the chicken, reserving the marinade, and stir-fry for 3 to 4 minutes, until no longer pink.
4. Toss in the scallion whites, garlic, and ginger and stir-fry for about 30 seconds. Pour in the marinade and mix to coat the chicken. Toss in the peanuts and cook for another 2 to 3 minutes, until the sauce becomes glossy.
5. Transfer to a serving plate, garnish with the scallion greens, and serve hot.

Broccoli Chicken

SERVES 4 ; PREP TIME: 15 MINUTES ; COOK TIME: 15 MINUTES

Broccoli chicken remains one of our go-to recipes of all time. As chefs, we seem to always have chicken and broccoli in the refrigerator, and if there is ginger lying around, we start the rice cooking before setting out to cook this dish. It's always satisfying and no one ever complains, "Broccoli chicken, again?"

1 tablespoon Shaoxing rice wine

2 teaspoons light soy sauce

1 teaspoon minced garlic

1 teaspoon cornstarch

¼ teaspoon sugar

¾ pound boneless, skinless chicken thighs, cut into 2-inch chunks

2 tablespoons vegetable oil

4 peeled fresh ginger slices, about the size of a quarter

Kosher salt

1 pound broccoli, cut into bite-size florets

2 tablespoons water

Red pepper flakes (optional)

¼ cup Black Bean Sauce or store-bought black bean sauce

1. In a small bowl, mix together the rice wine, light soy, garlic, cornstarch, and sugar. Add the chicken and marinate for 10 minutes.
2. Heat a wok over medium-high heat until a drop of water sizzles and evaporates on contact. Pour in the vegetable oil and swirl to coat the base of the wok. Add the ginger and a pinch of salt. Allow the ginger to sizzle for about 30 seconds, swirling gently.
3. Transfer the chicken to the wok, discarding the marinade. Stir-fry the chicken for 4 to 5 minutes, until no longer pink. Add the broccoli, water, and a pinch of red pepper flakes (if using) and stir-fry for 1 minute. Cover the wok and steam the broccoli for 6 to 8 minutes, until it is crisp-tender.
4. Stir in the black bean sauce until coated and heated through, about 2 minutes, or until the sauce has thickened slightly and become glossy.
5. Discard the ginger, transfer to a platter, and serve hot.

Cashew Chicken

SERVES 4 ; PREP TIME: 15 MINUTES ; COOK TIME: 5 MINUTES

Cashew Chicken is another Chinese American recipe that is unknown in China. It was created as a way of using local ingredients to adapt stir-fry dishes to American tastes. Invented in 1963 by David Leong, a Chinese American restaurateur from Springfield, Missouri, Cashew Chicken quickly became a popular take-out staple all over the United States and is still popular today.

2 tablespoons cooking oil

4 garlic cloves, crushed and chopped

1 tablespoon crushed and chopped ginger

1 medium carrot, roll-cut into 1-inch pieces

1 pound boneless chicken thighs, cut into ¼-inch pieces across the grain

4 ounces shiitake mushrooms, cut into ½-inch pieces

1 sweet red bell pepper, cut into 1-inch pieces

½ cup whole cashews

¼ cup oyster sauce

2 tablespoons soy sauce

4 scallions, cut diagonally into ¼-inch pieces

Rice or noodles, for serving

1. In a wok, heat the cooking oil over high heat until it begins to smoke.
2. Add the garlic, ginger, carrot, and chicken to the wok and stir-fry for 2 minutes.
3. Add the mushrooms and pepper to the wok and stir-fry for 1 minute.
4. Add the cashews and stir-fry for 1 minute.
5. Add the oyster sauce and soy sauce and stir-fry for 1 minute.
6. Add the scallions, toss until well combined, and serve over rice or noodles.

VARIATION TIP: Try different flavored cashews to vary this dish. One of my favorites is honey-roasted cashews for a slightly sweet flavor. Another option is to try coconut-crusted cashews.

Velvet Chicken and Snow Peas

SERVES 4 ; PREP TIME: 15 MINUTES ; COOK TIME: 10 MINUTES

Do you love chicken breasts but hate that they dry out when you stir-fry them? Then velveting is the technique for you. Chicken breasts are marinated in a combination of egg whites and cornstarch that tenderize and coat the chicken so that it stays tender during stir-frying.

2 large egg whites

2 tablespoons cornstarch, plus 1 teaspoon

¾ pound boneless, skinless chicken breasts, cut into bite-size slices

3½ tablespoons vegetable oil, divided

⅓ cup low-sodium chicken broth

1 tablespoon Shaoxing rice wine

Kosher salt

Ground white pepper

4 peeled fresh ginger slices, each about the size of a quarter

1 (4-ounce) can sliced bamboo shoots, rinsed and drained

3 garlic cloves, minced

¾ pound snow peas or sugar snap peas, strings removed

1. In a mixing bowl, using a fork or whisk, beat the egg whites until frothy and the tighter clumps of egg white are foamy. Stir in the 2 tablespoons of cornstarch until well blended and no longer clumpy. Fold in the chicken and 1 tablespoon of vegetable oil and marinate for 10 minutes or up to 30 minutes.
2. In a small bowl, stir together the chicken broth, rice wine, and remaining 1 teaspoon of cornstarch, and season with a pinch each of salt and white pepper. Set aside.
3. Bring a medium saucepan filled with water to a boil over high heat. Add ½ tablespoon of oil and reduce the heat to a simmer. Using a wok skimmer or slotted spoon to allow the marinade to drain off, transfer the chicken to the boiling water. Give the chicken a stir so that the pieces do not clump together. Cook for 40 to 50 seconds, until the chicken is white on the outside but not cooked through. Drain the chicken in a colander and shake off the excess water. Discard the simmering water.
4. Heat a wok over medium-high heat until a drop of water sizzles and evaporates on contact. Pour in the remaining 2 tablespoons of oil and swirl to coat the base of the wok. Season the oil by adding the ginger slices and salt. Allow the ginger to sizzle in the oil for about 30 seconds, swirling gently.
5. Add the bamboo shoots and garlic and, using a wok spatula, toss to coat with oil and cook until fragrant, about 30 seconds. Add the snow peas and stir-fry for about 2 minutes until bright green and crisp tender. Add the chicken to the wok and swirl in the sauce

mixture. Toss to coat and continue cooking for 1 to 2 minutes, until the chicken is completely cooked.

6. Transfer to a platter and discard the ginger. Serve hot.

SUBSTITUTION TIP: Any peas work with this recipe—shelled peas, sugar snap peas, frozen peas, fresh peas—you name it. Edamame is also a great green vegetable to toss into the wok if your supply of frozen peas is depleted.

Chicken and Vegetables with Black Bean Sauce

SERVES 4 ; PREP TIME: 15 MINUTES ; COOK TIME: 10 MINUTES

Don't be fooled by the list of ingredients. This recipe is very simple to knock together. As the chicken is marinating, you can prep the vegetables and steam some rice. Dinner will come together in less than half an hour.

1 tablespoon light soy sauce

1 teaspoon sesame oil

1 teaspoon cornstarch

¾ pound boneless, skinless chicken thighs, cut into bite-size pieces

3 tablespoons vegetable oil, divided

1 peeled fresh ginger slice, about the size of a quarter

Kosher salt

1 small yellow onion, cut into bite-size pieces

½ red bell pepper, cut into bite-size pieces

½ yellow or green bell pepper, cut into bite-size pieces

3 garlic cloves, chopped

⅓ cup Black Bean Sauce or store-bought black bean sauce

1. In a large bowl, stir the light soy, sesame oil, and cornstarch together until the cornstarch dissolves. Add the chicken and toss to coat in the marinade. Set the chicken aside to marinate for 10 minutes.
2. Heat a wok over medium-high heat until a drop of water sizzles and evaporates on contact. Pour in 2 tablespoons of vegetable oil and swirl to coat the base of the wok. Season the oil by adding the ginger and a pinch of salt. Allow the ginger to sizzle in the oil for about 30 seconds, swirling gently.
3. Transfer the chicken to the wok and discard the marinade. Let the pieces sear in the wok for 2 to 3 minutes. Flip to sear on the other side for another 1 to 2 minutes more. Stir-fry by tossing and flipping around in the wok quickly for 1 more minute. Transfer to a clean bowl.
4. Add the remaining 1 tablespoon of oil and toss in the onion and bell peppers. Quickly stir-fry for 2 to 3 minutes, tossing and flipping the vegetables with a wok spatula until the onion looks translucent but is still firm in texture. Add the garlic and stir-fry for another 30 seconds.
5. Return the chicken to the wok and add the black bean sauce. Toss and flip until the chicken and vegetables are coated.
6. Transfer to a platter, discard the ginger, and serve hot.

PREP TIP: You can change out the vegetables to use whatever you like or have on hand. Just make sure to keep the pieces thinly sliced or cut into small, bite-size pieces. As long as the pieces are uniform in size and fairly small, the food will cook quickly and evenly over medium-high heat.

Chicken in Sesame Sauce

SERVES 4 ; PREP TIME: 15 MINUTES ; COOK TIME: 15 MINUTES

Sesame oil is a magical ingredient. Its unmistakably mouthwatering aroma can elevate the simplest dish. Don't skimp on it—you can never have too much sesame oil! If you like, toss in a couple of handfuls of sugar snap peas for extra vegetables and a pop of fresh green in this dish. Served over rice, this homey dish is so satisfying.

3 large egg whites

3 tablespoons cornstarch, divided

1½ tablespoons light soy sauce, divided

1 pound boneless, skinless chicken thighs, cut into bite-size pieces

3 cups vegetable oil

3 peeled fresh ginger slices, each about the size of a quarter

Kosher salt

Red pepper flakes

3 garlic cloves, coarsely chopped

¼ cup low-sodium chicken broth

2 tablespoons sesame oil

2 scallions, thinly sliced, for garnish

1 tablespoon sesame seeds, for garnish

1. In a mixing bowl, using a fork or whisk, beat the egg whites until frothy and the tighter clumps of egg white are foamy. Stir together 2 tablespoons of cornstarch and 2 teaspoons of light soy until well blended. Fold in the chicken and marinate for 10 minutes.
2. Pour the oil into the wok; the oil should be about 1 to 1½ inches deep. Bring the oil to 375°F over medium-high heat. You can tell the oil is at the right temperature when you dip the end of a wooden spoon into the oil. If the oil bubbles and sizzles around it, the oil is ready.
3. Using a slotted spoon or wok skimmer, lift the chicken from the marinade and shake off the excess. Carefully lower into the hot oil. Fry the chicken in batches for 3 to 4 minutes, or until the chicken is golden brown and crispy on the surface. Transfer to a paper towel–lined plate.
4. Pour out all but 1 tablespoon of oil from the wok and set it over medium-high heat. Swirl the oil to coat the base of the wok. Season the oil by adding the ginger and a pinch of salt and red pepper flakes. Allow the ginger and pepper flakes to sizzle in the oil for about 30 seconds, swirling gently.

5. Add the garlic and stir-fry, tossing and flipping with a wok spatula for 30 seconds. Stir in the chicken broth, remaining 2½ teaspoons of light soy, and remaining 1 tablespoon of cornstarch. Simmer for 4 to 5 minutes, until the sauce thickens and becomes glossy. Add the sesame oil and stir to combine.
6. Turn off the heat and add the fried chicken, tossing to coat with the sauce. Remove the ginger and discard. Transfer to a platter and garnish with the sliced scallions and sesame seeds.

SUBSTITUTION TIP: Cut up some pork belly and substitute that for the chicken. Sesame pork is a revelation!

Sweet-and-Sour Chicken

SERVES 4 ; PREP TIME: 10 MINUTES ; COOK TIME: 15 MINUTES

Look no further than this dish to see how cross-cultural dishes influence each other. Here we have traditional Chinese ingredients, as well as tropical pineapple and American ketchup, and it all works together for a well-balanced, zesty dish that is a Chinese-American classic.

2 teaspoons cornstarch

2 tablespoons water

3 tablespoons vegetable oil, divided

4 peeled fresh ginger slices, each about the size of a quarter

Kosher salt

¾ pound boneless, skinless chicken thighs, cut into bite-size chunks

½ red bell pepper, cut into ½-inch pieces

½ green bell pepper, cut into ½-inch pieces

½ yellow onion, cut into ½-inch pieces

1 (8-ounce) can pineapple chunks, drained, juices reserved

1 (4-ounce) can sliced water chestnuts, drained

¼ cup low-sodium chicken broth

2 tablespoons light brown sugar

2 tablespoons apple cider vinegar

2 tablespoons ketchup

1 teaspoon Worcestershire sauce

3 scallions, thinly sliced, for garnish

1. In a small bowl, stir together the cornstarch and water and set aside.
2. Heat a wok over medium-high heat until a drop of water sizzles and evaporates on contact. Pour in 2 tablespoons of oil and swirl to coat the base of the wok. Season the oil by adding the ginger and a pinch of salt. Allow the ginger to sizzle in the oil for about 30 seconds, swirling gently.
3. Add the chicken and sear against the wok for 2 to 3 minutes. Flip and toss the chicken, stir-frying for about 1 minute more, or until no longer pink. Transfer to a bowl and set aside.
4. Add the remaining 1 tablespoon of oil and swirl to coat. Stir-fry the red and green bell peppers and onion for 3 to 4 minutes, until soft and translucent. Add the pineapple and water chestnuts and continue to stir-fry for another minute. Add the vegetables to the chicken and set aside.

5. Pour the reserved pineapple juice, chicken broth, brown sugar, vinegar, ketchup, and Worcestershire sauce into the wok and bring to a boil. Keep the heat on medium-high and cook for about 4 minutes, until the liquid is reduced by half.
6. Return the chicken and vegetables to the wok and toss to combine with the sauce. Give the cornstarch-water mixture a quick stir and add to the wok. Toss and flip everything around until the cornstarch begins to thicken the sauce, becoming glossy.
7. Discard the ginger, transfer to a platter, garnish with the scallions, and serve hot.

SUBSTITUTION TIP: Instead of chicken, make sweet-and-sour pork or sweet-and-sour shrimp. Apply your newly minted velveting skills to the pork and shrimp and turn this dish into something really special.

Moo Goo Gai Pan

SERVES 4 ; PREP TIME: 20 MINUTES ; COOK TIME: 15 MINUTES

"Fresh mushrooms with sliced chicken" is the direct translation from Cantonese for Moo Goo Gai Pan. When we think of stir-fried chicken with mushrooms, this dish comes to mind. We add crunchy elements like bamboo shoots and water chestnuts to enhance the texture.

1 tablespoon light soy sauce

1 tablespoon Shaoxing rice wine

2 teaspoons sesame oil

¾ pound boneless, skinless chicken breasts, sliced into thin strips

½ cup low-sodium chicken broth

2 tablespoons oyster sauce

1 teaspoon sugar

1 tablespoon cornstarch

3 tablespoons vegetable oil, divided

4 peeled fresh ginger slices, each about the size of a quarter

Kosher salt

4 ounces fresh button mushrooms, thinly sliced

1 (4-ounce) can sliced bamboo shoots, drained

1 (4-ounce) can sliced water chestnuts, drained

1 garlic clove, finely minced

1. In a large bowl, whisk together the light soy, rice wine, and sesame oil until smooth. Add the chicken and toss to coat. Marinate for 15 minutes.
2. In a small bowl, whisk together chicken broth, oyster sauce, sugar, and cornstarch until smooth and set aside.
3. Heat a wok over medium-high heat until a drop of water sizzles and evaporates on contact. Pour in 2 tablespoons of vegetable oil and swirl to coat the base of the wok. Season the oil by adding the ginger and a small pinch of salt. Allow the ginger to sizzle in the oil for about 30 seconds, swirling gently.
4. Add the chicken and discard the marinade. Stir-fry for 2 to 3 minutes, until the chicken is no longer pink. Transfer to a clean bowl and set aside.
5. Add the remaining 1 tablespoon of vegetable oil. Stir-fry the mushrooms for 3 to 4 minutes, tossing and flipping quickly. As soon as the mushrooms become dry, stop stir-frying and let the mushrooms sit against the hot wok for about a minute. Toss again and then rest again for another minute.

6. Add the bamboo shoots, water chestnuts, and garlic. Stir-fry for 1 minute, or until the garlic is fragrant. Return the chicken to the wok and toss to combine.
7. Stir the sauce together and add to the wok. Stir-fry and cook until the sauce begins to boil, about 45 seconds. Keep tossing and flipping until the sauce thickens and becomes glossy. Remove the ginger and discard. Transfer to a platter and serve while hot.

SUBSTITUTION TIP: If you have access to wild mushrooms, use them to give a deeper, earthier quality to the dish.

Egg Foo Yong

SERVES 4 ; PREP TIME: 15 MINUTES ; COOK TIME: 15 MINUTES

Truthfully, there isn't really a standard recipe for egg foo yong. It's really a "kitchen sink" kind of dish. According to folklore, egg foo yong was created by Chinese cooks during the California Gold Rush. Whatever egg foo yong's origins, our take on this classic is one your family is sure to love.

5 large eggs, at room temperature

Kosher salt

Ground white pepper

½ cup thinly sliced shiitake mushroom caps

½ cup frozen peas, thawed

2 scallions, chopped

2 teaspoons sesame oil

½ cup low-sodium chicken broth

1½ tablespoons oyster sauce

1 tablespoon Shaoxing rice wine

½ teaspoon sugar

2 tablespoons light soy sauce

1 tablespoon cornstarch

3 tablespoons vegetable oil

Cooked rice, for serving

1. In a large bowl, whisk the eggs with a pinch each of salt and white pepper. Stir in the mushrooms, peas, scallions, and sesame oil. Set aside.
2. Make the sauce by simmering the chicken broth, oyster sauce, rice wine, and sugar in a small saucepan over medium heat. In a small glass measuring cup, whisk the light soy and cornstarch until the cornstarch is completely dissolved. Pour the cornstarch mixture into the sauce while whisking constantly and cook for 3 to 4 minutes, until the sauce becomes thick enough to coat the back of the spoon. Cover and set aside.
3. Heat a wok over medium-high heat until a drop of water sizzles and evaporates on contact. Pour in the vegetable oil and swirl to coat the base of the wok. Add the egg mixture and cook, swirling and shaking the wok until the bottom side is golden. Slide the omelet out of the pan onto a plate and invert over the wok or turn over with a spatula to cook the other side until golden. Slide the omelet out onto a serving platter and serve over cooked rice with a spoonful of sauce.

Green Bean Chicken

SERVES 4 ; PREP TIME: 15 MINUTES ; COOK TIME: 15 MINUTES

Chicken, green beans, and almonds go really well together, so why not give it a Chinese twist? One of the beautiful things about wok cooking is that a little bit of protein can go a long way. It's perfect for stretching your food dollars while still eating well.

¾ pound boneless, skinless chicken thighs, sliced across the grain into bite-size strips

3 tablespoons Shaoxing rice wine, divided

2 teaspoons cornstarch

Kosher salt

Red pepper flakes

3 tablespoons vegetable oil, divided

4 peeled fresh ginger slices, each about the size of a quarter

¾ pound green beans, trimmed and halved crosswise diagonally

2 tablespoons light soy sauce

1 tablespoon seasoned rice vinegar

¼ cup slivered almonds, toasted

2 teaspoons sesame oil

1. In a mixing bowl, combine the chicken with 1 tablespoon of rice wine, cornstarch, a small pinch of salt, and a pinch of red pepper flakes. Stir to evenly coat the chicken. Marinate for 10 minutes.
2. Heat a wok over medium-high heat until a drop of water sizzles and evaporates on contact. Pour in 2 tablespoons of vegetable oil and swirl to coat the base of the wok. Season the oil by adding the ginger and a small pinch of salt. Allow the ginger to sizzle in the oil for about 30 seconds, swirling gently.
3. Add the chicken and marinade to the wok and stir-fry for 3 to 4 minutes, or until the chicken is slightly seared and no longer pink. Transfer to a clean bowl and set aside.
4. Add the remaining 1 tablespoon of vegetable oil and stir-fry the green beans for 2 to 3 minutes, or until they turn bright green. Return the chicken to the wok and toss together. Add the remaining 2 tablespoons of rice wine, light soy, and vinegar. Toss to combine and coat and allow the green beans to simmer for 3 more minutes, or until the green beans are tender. Remove the ginger and discard.
5. Toss the almonds in and transfer to a platter. Drizzle with the sesame oil and serve hot.

SERVING TIP: For a nuttier-tasting dish, serve with steamed brown rice instead of white rice.

Teriyaki Chicken and Vegetables

SERVES 4 ; PREP TIME: 15 MINUTES ; COOK TIME: 5 MINUTES

Teriyaki is a Japanese cooking technique in which ingredients are stir-fried in a glaze of tamari or soy sauce, mirin, and sugar. The word teriyaki comes from the word teri which means "glaze" and yaki which means "cooking or grilling with high heat." The searing heat caramelizes both the natural and added sugars, forming the glaze.

½ pound boneless chicken thighs, cut across the grain into ⅛-inch pieces

1 tablespoon cornstarch

1 tablespoon mirin

1 tablespoon rice vinegar

2 tablespoons tamari or soy sauce

¼ cup honey

1 teaspoon sesame oil

2 tablespoons cooking oil

2 garlic cloves, crushed and chopped

1 tablespoon crushed and chopped ginger

1 medium onion, diced into 1-inch pieces

1 red bell pepper, diced into 1-inch pieces

4 ounces shiitake mushrooms, sliced

4 scallions, cut diagonally in ¼-inch pieces

Rice or noodles, for serving

1. In a large bowl, combine the chicken, cornstarch, mirin, vinegar, tamari, honey, and sesame oil.
2. In a wok, heat the cooking oil over high heat until it begins to smoke.
3. Add the garlic, ginger, and chicken and stir-fry for 1 minute.
4. Add the onion, red bell pepper, and mushrooms and stir-fry for 1 minute.
5. Add the scallions, toss, and serve over rice or noodles.

VARIATION TIP: Try using maple syrup or molasses instead of honey as a sweetener.

Tomato Egg Stir-Fry

SERVES 4 ; PREP TIME: 5 MINUTES ; COOK TIME: 10 MINUTES

This popular late-night dish in our houses uses ingredients that we always have on hand. Fast and easy to make, this dish is equally good over rice or noodles.

4 large eggs, at room temperature

1 teaspoon Shaoxing rice wine

½ teaspoon sesame oil

½ teaspoon kosher salt

Freshly ground black pepper

3 tablespoons vegetable oil, divided

2 peeled fresh ginger slices, each about the size of a quarter

1 pound grape or cherry tomatoes

1 teaspoon sugar

Cooked rice or noodles, for serving

1. In a large bowl, whisk the eggs. Add the rice wine, sesame oil, salt, and a pinch of pepper and continue whisking until just combined.
2. Heat a wok over medium-high heat until a drop of water sizzles and evaporates on contact. Pour in 2 tablespoons of vegetable oil and swirl to coat the base of the wok. Swirl the egg mixture into the hot wok. Swirl and shake the eggs to cook. Transfer the eggs to a serving plate when just cooked but not dry. Tent with foil to keep warm.
3. Add the remaining 1 tablespoon of vegetable oil to the wok. Season the oil by adding the ginger and a pinch of salt. Allow the ginger to sizzle in the oil for about 30 seconds, swirling gently.
4. Toss in the tomatoes and sugar, stirring to coat with the oil. Cover and cook for about 5 minutes, stirring occasionally, until the tomatoes are soft and have released their juices. Discard the ginger slices and season the tomatoes with salt and pepper.
5. Spoon the tomatoes over the eggs, and serve over cooked rice or noodles.

SUBSTITUTION TIP: We use grape or cherry tomatoes here for easy prep and flavor. No chopping is required, and the smaller tomatoes tend to taste sweet year-round. But feel free to substitute garden-ripe tomatoes, if you have them.

Shrimp and Scrambled Eggs

SERVES 4 ; PREP TIME: 15 MINUTES ; COOK TIME: 10 MINUTES

The secret to sweet, succulent shrimp is to brine them before cooking. The simple step of soaking raw shrimp in a sugar-salt solution enhances the shrimp's flavor and also protects it from overcooking. If you have the time to brine shrimp in all recipes using shrimp, we really recommend it.

2 tablespoons kosher salt, plus more for seasoning

2 tablespoons sugar

2 cups cold water

6 ounces medium shrimp (U41–50), peeled and deveined

4 large eggs, at room temperature

½ teaspoon sesame oil

Freshly ground black pepper

2 tablespoons vegetable oil, divided

2 peeled fresh ginger slices, each about the size of a quarter

2 garlic cloves, thinly sliced

1 bunch chives, cut into ½-inch pieces

1. In a large bowl, whisk the salt and sugar into the water until they dissolve. Add the shrimp to the brine. Cover and refrigerate for 10 minutes.
2. Drain the shrimp in a colander and rinse. Discard the brine. Spread the shrimp out on a paper towel–lined baking sheet and pat dry.
3. In another large bowl, whisk the eggs with the sesame oil and a pinch each of salt and pepper until combined. Set aside.
4. Heat a wok over medium-high heat until a drop of water sizzles and evaporates on contact. Pour in 1 tablespoon of vegetable oil and swirl to coat the base of the wok. Season the oil by adding the ginger and a pinch of salt. Allow the ginger to sizzle in the oil for about 30 seconds, swirling gently.
5. Add the garlic and stir-fry briefly to flavor the oil, about 10 seconds. Do not let the garlic brown or burn. Add the shrimp and stir-fry for about 2 minutes, until they turn pink. Transfer to a plate and discard the ginger.
6. Return the wok to the heat and add the remaining 1 tablespoon of vegetable oil. When the oil is hot, swirl the egg mixture into the wok. Swirl and shake the eggs to cook. Add the chives to the pan and continue cooking until eggs are cooked but not dry. Return the shrimp to the pan and toss to combine. Transfer to a serving plate.

PRO TIP: Keep frozen shrimp and a supply of eggs on hand at all times. That way, when you need a quick and easy dinner idea, you always have these available, making this the perfect last-minute "Oops, I forgot to plan for dinner" plan.

Savory Steamed Egg Custard

SERVES 4 ; PREP TIME: 10 MINUTES ; COOK TIME: 10 MINUTES

Soft, silky, and comforting—that's what comes to mind when we think of steamed egg custard. This is a fantastic starter to Sunday brunch or perfect for a light supper. We like to use individual ramekins, but if you don't have them, cook the custard in a glass pie dish and serve it family style instead. If you want, place a few thin slices of vegetables in dishes before pouring in the egg mixture.

4 large eggs, at room temperature

1¾ cups low-sodium chicken broth or filtered water

2 teaspoons Shaoxing rice wine

½ teaspoon kosher salt

2 scallions, green part only, thinly sliced

4 teaspoons sesame oil

1. In a large bowl, whisk the eggs. Add the broth and rice wine and whisk to combine. Strain the egg mixture through a fine-mesh sieve set over a liquid measuring cup to remove air bubbles. Pour the egg mixture into 4 (6-ounce) ramekins. With a paring knife, pop any bubbles on the surface of the egg mixture. Cover the ramekins with aluminum foil.
2. Rinse a bamboo steamer basket and its lid under cold water and place it in the wok. Pour in 2 inches of water, or until it comes above the bottom rim of the steamer by ¼ to ½ inch, but not so much that it touches the bottom of the basket. Place the ramekins in the steamer basket. Cover with the lid.
3. Bring the water to a boil, then reduce the heat to a low simmer. Steam over low heat for about 10 minutes or until the eggs are just set.
4. Carefully remove the ramekins from the steamer and garnish each custard with some scallions and a few drops of sesame oil. Serve immediately.

PREP TIP: Straining the egg mixture in this recipe is the secret to removing bubbles and creating a silky texture. Don't skip it; it is absolutely worth the extra step.

BEEF, PORK, AND LAMB

Beef and Chinese Broccoli with Oyster Sauce

SERVES 4 ; PREP TIME: 15 MINUTES ; COOK TIME: 5 MINUTES

Gai lan, also known as Chinese broccoli or Chinese kale, has glossy leaves, thick stems, and florets like Western broccoli. It has a stronger flavor than Western broccoli and stands up well to heavier flavors such as oyster sauce. Broccolini is like gai lan. In some larger groceries, all three are available, but gai lan can be found consistently in Asian markets.

½ pound thin-sliced rib eye, cut across the grain into ⅛-inch matchsticks

1 tablespoon cornstarch

1 tablespoon Shaoxing rice wine

1 tablespoon soy sauce

2 tablespoons cooking oil

2 garlic cloves, crushed and chopped

1 tablespoon crushed and chopped ginger

2 cups Chinese broccoli (gai lan) or regular broccoli florets, cut into 1-inch pieces

¼ cup oyster sauce

4 scallions, cut diagonally into ¼-inch pieces

Rice or noodles, for serving

1. In a medium bowl, combine the steak, cornstarch, wine, and soy sauce and mix well.
2. In a wok, heat the cooking oil over high heat until it begins to smoke.
3. Add the garlic, ginger, and beef and stir-fry for 1 minute, or until the garlic and ginger are fragrant.
4. Add the broccoli and stir-fry for 1 minute, or until it is lightly coated with oil.
5. Add the oyster sauce and stir-fry for 1 minute, or until all the ingredients are coated with the sauce.
6. Add the scallions, toss, and serve over rice or noodles.

VARIATION TIP: If you need to avoid shellfish, you can substitute hoisin, plum, or black bean sauce for the oyster sauce.

Sesame Beef

SERVES 4 ; PREP TIME: 15 MINUTES ; COOK TIME: 10 MINUTES

Sesame is a strong, nutty, savory aromatic that pairs well with beef. We've brightened it up with orange juice in the sauce that brings the sesame and beef flavors together. Choose this recipe when you have friends coming over. As soon as your guests get a whiff of the sesame oil, they'll praise you for being a culinary genius!

1 tablespoon light soy sauce

2 tablespoons sesame oil, divided

2 teaspoons cornstarch, divided

1 pound hanger, skirt, or flat iron steak, cut into ¼-inch-thick strips

½ cup freshly squeezed orange juice

½ teaspoon rice vinegar

1 teaspoon sriracha (optional)

1 teaspoon light brown sugar

Kosher salt

Freshly ground black pepper

3 tablespoons vegetable oil, divided

4 peeled fresh ginger slices, each about the size of a quarter

1 small yellow onion, thinly sliced

3 garlic cloves, minced

½ tablespoon white sesame seeds, for garnish

1. In a large bowl, stir together the light soy, 1 tablespoon of sesame oil, and 1 teaspoon of cornstarch until the cornstarch dissolves. Add the beef and toss to coat in the marinade. Set aside to marinate for 10 minutes while you prep the sauce.
2. In a glass measuring cup, stir together the orange juice, remaining 1 tablespoon of sesame oil, rice vinegar, sriracha (if using), brown sugar, remaining 1 teaspoon of cornstarch, and a pinch each of salt and pepper. Stir until the cornstarch is dissolved and set aside.
3. Heat a wok over medium-high heat until a drop of water sizzles and evaporates on contact. Pour in 2 tablespoons of vegetable oil and swirl to coat the base of the wok. Season the oil by adding the ginger and a pinch of salt. Allow the ginger to sizzle in the oil for about 30 seconds, swirling gently.
4. Using tongs, transfer the beef to the wok and discard the marinade. Let the pieces sear in the wok for 2 to 3 minutes. Flip to sear on the other side for another 1 to 2 minutes. Stir-fry by tossing and flipping around in the wok quickly for 1 more minute. Transfer to a clean bowl.

5. Add the remaining 1 tablespoon of vegetable oil and toss in the onion. Quickly stir-fry, tossing and flipping the onion with a wok spatula for 2 to 3 minutes, until the onion looks translucent but is still firm in texture. Add the garlic and stir-fry for another 30 seconds.
6. Swirl in the sauce and continue to cook until the sauce starts to thicken. Return the beef to the wok, tossing and flipping so the beef and onion are coated with sauce. Season to taste with salt and pepper.
7. Transfer to a platter, discard the ginger, sprinkle with the sesame seeds, and serve hot.

SUBSTITUTION TIP: We love hanger, skirt, or flat iron steak for this recipe because of the flavor and texture. If you can't find one of these at your local market you can substitute flank steak.

Mongolian Beef

SERVES 4 ; PREP TIME: 15 MINUTES ; COOK TIME: 10 MINUTES

Mongolian beef originated not in Mongolia, but in Taiwan. It gained popularity in Chinese-American restaurants thanks to its sweet-spicy balance. If spicy food isn't your thing, you can back down on the chilies. Marinating the beef longer makes it more delicious, but because it's sliced so thin, don't marinate more than 30 minutes or the beef will become too salty.

2 tablespoons Shaoxing rice wine

1 tablespoon dark soy sauce

1 tablespoon cornstarch, divided

¾ pound flank steak, cut against the grain into ¼-inch-thick slices

¼ cup low-sodium chicken broth

1 tablespoon light brown sugar

1 cup vegetable oil

4 or 5 whole dried red Chinese chilies

4 garlic cloves, coarsely chopped

1 teaspoon peeled finely minced fresh ginger

½ yellow onion, thinly sliced

2 tablespoons coarsely chopped fresh cilantro

1. In a mixing bowl, stir together the rice wine, dark soy, and 1 tablespoon of cornstarch. Add the sliced flank steak and toss to coat. Set aside and marinate for 10 minutes.
2. Pour the oil into a wok and bring it to 375°F over medium-high heat. You can tell the oil is at the right temperature when you dip the end of a wooden spoon into the oil. If the oil bubbles and sizzles around it, the oil is ready.
3. Lift the beef from the marinade, reserving the marinade. Add the beef to the oil and fry for 2 to 3 minutes, until it develops a golden crust. Using a wok skimmer, transfer the beef to a clean bowl and set aside. Add the chicken broth and brown sugar to the marinade bowl and stir to combine.
4. Pour out all but 1 tablespoon of oil from the wok and set it over medium-high heat. Add the chili peppers, garlic, and ginger. Allow the aromatics to sizzle in the oil for about 10 seconds, swirling gently.
5. Add the onion and stir-fry for 1 to 2 minutes, or until the onion is soft and translucent. Add the chicken broth mixture and toss to combine. Simmer for about 2 minutes, then add the beef and toss everything together for another 30 seconds.
6. Transfer to a platter, garnish with the cilantro, and serve hot.

VARIATION TIP: You can make the dish spicier by adding sliced fresh red chilies when stir-frying the onions.

Sichuan Beef with Celery and Carrots

SERVES 4 ; PREP TIME: 20 MINUTES ; COOK TIME: 10 MINUTES

This recipe is a great example of how thinly sliced, uniform-size ingredients can cook quickly in a hot wok. Save yourself even more time by picking up precut vegetables at the store. Served over cooked rice, it's a perfectly balanced meal that can be on your table in less than 30 minutes.

2 tablespoons Shaoxing rice wine

1 tablespoon dark soy sauce

2 teaspoons sesame oil

¾ pound flank or skirt steak, cut against the grain into ¼-inch-thick slices

1 tablespoon hoisin sauce

2 teaspoons light soy sauce

2 teaspoons water

2 tablespoons cornstarch, divided

¼ teaspoon Chinese five spice powder

2 tablespoons vegetable oil

1 teaspoon Sichuan peppercorns, crushed

4 peeled fresh ginger slices, each about the size of a quarter

3 garlic cloves, lightly crushed

2 celery stalks, julienned to 3-inch strips

1 large carrot, peeled and julienned to 3-inch strips

2 scallions, thinly sliced

1. In a mixing bowl, stir together the rice wine, dark soy, and sesame oil. Add the beef and toss to combine. Set aside for 10 minutes. In a small bowl, combine the hoisin sauce, light soy, water, 1 tablespoon of cornstarch, and five spice powder. Set aside.
2. Heat a wok over medium-high heat until a drop of water sizzles and evaporates on contact. Pour in the vegetable oil and swirl to coat the base of the wok. Season the oil by adding the peppercorns, ginger, and garlic. Allow the aromatics to sizzle in the oil for about 10 seconds, swirling gently.
3. Toss the beef in the remaining 1 tablespoon of cornstarch to coat, and add to the wok. Sear the beef against the side of the wok for 1 to 2 minutes, or until a golden-brown seared crust develops. Flip and sear on the other side for another minute. Toss and flip for about 2 minutes more, until the beef is no longer pink.
4. Move the beef to the sides of the wok and add the celery and carrot to the center. Stir-fry, tossing and flipping until the vegetables are tender, another 2 to 3 minutes. Stir the hoisin sauce mixture and pour into the wok. Continue to stir-fry, coating the beef and

vegetables with the sauce for 1 to 2 minutes, until the sauce begins to thicken and becomes glossy. Remove the ginger and garlic and discard.

5. Transfer to a platter and garnish with the scallions. Serve hot.

SUBSTITUTION TIP: The Sichuan peppercorns will give your dish an authentic spicy flavor. If you don't have them in your pantry, substitute a blend of small pinches of red pepper flakes, cracked black peppercorns, and ground white pepper.

Tomato and Beef Stir-Fry

SERVES 4 ; PREP TIME: 15 MINUTES ; COOK TIME: 10 MINUTES

Tomatoes and beef make a fantastic combination. We encourage you to make this dish when tomatoes are at their peak—and homegrown tomatoes are the best. Served over a steaming bowl of white rice, this dish just can't be beat.

¾ pound flank or skirt steak, cut against the grain into ¼-inch-thick slices

1½ tablespoons cornstarch, divided

1 tablespoon Shaoxing rice wine

Kosher salt

Ground white pepper

1 tablespoon tomato paste

2 tablespoons light soy sauce

1 teaspoon sesame oil

1 teaspoon sugar

2 tablespoons water

2 tablespoons vegetable oil

4 peeled fresh ginger slices, each about the size of a quarter

1 large shallot, thinly sliced

2 garlic cloves, finely minced

5 large tomatoes, each cut into 6 wedges

2 scallions, white and green parts separated, thinly sliced

1. In a small bowl, mix the beef with 1 tablespoon of cornstarch, rice wine, and a small pinch each of salt and white pepper. Set aside for 10 minutes.
2. In another small bowl, stir together the remaining ½ tablespoon of cornstarch, tomato paste, light soy, sesame oil, sugar, and water. Set aside.
3. Heat a wok over medium-high heat until a drop of water sizzles and evaporates on contact. Pour in the vegetable oil and swirl to coat the base of the wok. Season the oil by adding the ginger and a pinch of salt. Allow the ginger to sizzle in the oil for about 30 seconds, swirling gently.
4. Transfer the beef to the wok and stir-fry for 3 to 4 minutes, until no longer pink. Add the shallot and garlic and stir-fry for 1 minute. Add the tomatoes and scallion whites and continue to stir-fry for another 2 to 3 minutes, or until the tomatoes begin to break down slightly.
5. Stir in the sauce and continue to stir-fry for 1 to 2 minutes, or until the beef and tomatoes are coated and the sauce has thickened slightly.

6.Discard the ginger, transfer to a platter, and garnish with the scallion greens. Serve hot.

PREP TIP: Thinner cuts of beef like flank or skirt steak are more economical but can be challenging to slice thin. Skip the struggle and put the meat in the freezer for about 20 minutes, or until slightly frozen. The steaks will be much easier to slice.

Beef and Broccoli

SERVES 4 ; PREP TIME: 15 MINUTES ; COOK TIME: 20 MINUTES

Tender and tangy broccoli beef over steamed rice hits the spot when you're craving Chinese food. It's the perfect balance of sweet hoisin sauce and umami-packed oyster sauce. The secret to really tender beef strips is to marinate them in baking soda before cooking.

¾ pound skirt steak, cut across the grain into ¼-inch-thick slices

1 tablespoon baking soda

1 tablespoon cornstarch

4 tablespoons water, divided

2 tablespoons oyster sauce

2 tablespoons Shaoxing rice wine

2 teaspoons light brown sugar

1 tablespoon hoisin sauce

2 tablespoons vegetable oil

4 peeled fresh ginger slices, about the size of a quarter

Kosher salt

1 pound broccoli, cut into bite-size florets

2 garlic cloves, finely minced

1. In a small bowl, mix together the beef and baking soda to coat. Set aside for 10 minutes. Rinse the beef extremely well and then pat it dry with paper towels.
2. In another small bowl, stir the cornstarch with 2 tablespoons of water and mix in the oyster sauce, rice wine, brown sugar, and hoisin sauce. Set aside.
3. Heat a wok over medium-high heat until a drop of water sizzles and evaporates on contact. Pour in the oil and swirl to coat the base of the wok. Season the oil by adding the ginger and a pinch of salt. Allow the ginger to sizzle in the oil for about 30 seconds, swirling gently. Add the beef to the wok and stir-fry for 3 to 4 minutes, until no longer pink. Transfer the beef to a bowl and set aside.
4. Add the broccoli and garlic and stir-fry for 1 minute, then add the remaining 2 tablespoons of water. Cover the wok and steam the broccoli for 6 to 8 minutes, until it is crisp-tender.
5. Return the beef to the wok and stir in the sauce for 2 to 3 minutes, until fully coated and the sauce has thickened slightly. Discard the ginger, transfer to a platter, and serve hot.

Black Pepper Beef Stir-Fry

SERVES 4 ; PREP TIME: 15 MINUTES ; COOK TIME: 10 MINUTES

If you are searching for a deeply satisfying and spicy beef stir-fry, look no further! The savory quality of the oyster sauce enhances and stands up to the sharpness of the black pepper at the end. Cook lots of rice for this—you'll need it to balance the dish.

1 tablespoon oyster sauce

1 tablespoon Shaoxing rice wine

2 teaspoons cornstarch

2 teaspoons light soy sauce

Ground white pepper

¼ teaspoon sugar

¾ pound beef tenderloin tips or sirloin tips, cut into 1-inch pieces

3 tablespoons vegetable oil

3 peeled fresh ginger slices, each about the size of a quarter

Kosher salt

1 green bell pepper, cut into ½-inch-wide strips

1 small red onion, thinly sliced into strips

1 teaspoon freshly ground black pepper, or more to taste

2 teaspoons sesame oil

1. In a mixing bowl, stir together the oyster sauce, rice wine, cornstarch, light soy, a pinch of white pepper, and sugar. Toss the beef to coat and marinate for 10 minutes.
2. Heat a wok over medium-high heat until a drop of water sizzles and evaporates on contact. Pour in the vegetable oil and swirl to coat the base of the wok. Add the ginger and a pinch of salt. Allow the ginger to sizzle in the oil for about 30 seconds, swirling gently.
3. Using tongs, transfer the beef to the wok and discard any remaining marinade. Sear against the wok for 1 to 2 minutes, or until a brown seared crust develops. Flip the beef and sear on the other side, another 2 minutes more. Stir-fry, tossing and flipping in the wok for another 1 to 2 minutes, then transfer the beef to a clean bowl.
4. Add the bell pepper and onion and stir-fry for 2 to 3 minutes, or until the vegetables look shiny and tender. Return the beef to the wok, add the black pepper, and stir-fry together for 1 more minute.
5. Discard the ginger, transfer to a platter, and drizzle the sesame oil on top. Serve hot.

Thai Basil Beef and Peppers

SERVES 4 ; PREP TIME: 15 MINUTES ; COOK TIME: 5 MINUTES

Fresh Thai basil really adds to the complex umami flavor of fish and soy sauce in this beef stir-fry. Widely used throughout Southeast Asia, Thai basil's flavor is often described as anise- or licorice-like and slightly spicy. It stands up well to stir-frying, with its small, narrow leaves, purple stems, and pink-purple flowers.

2 tablespoons cooking oil

1 tablespoon crushed and chopped ginger

2 garlic cloves, crushed and chopped

1 pound ground beef

1 medium red bell pepper, cut into ½-inch pieces

1 tablespoon fish sauce

1 tablespoon soy sauce

2 tablespoons brown sugar

1 cup fresh Thai basil leaves, coarsely chopped

Steamed rice, for serving

1. In a wok, heat the cooking oil over high heat until it shimmers.
2. Add the ginger, garlic, and ground beef to the wok and stir-fry for 2 minutes.
3. Add the red bell pepper, fish sauce, soy sauce, and sugar to the wok and stir-fry for 1 minute.
4. Add the basil leaves and let them just wilt in the wok. Serve over steamed rice.

VARIATION TIP: A wedge of lime for each bowl provides a nice contrast to the sweet and salty flavor of the sauces and brown sugar. Serve on the side and squeeze atop the dish just before eating.

Hoisin Beef Lettuce Cups

SERVES 4 ; PREP TIME: 15 MINUTES ; COOK TIME: 15 MINUTES

We've had versions of this dish at many Hong Kong–style restaurants over the years. In Cantonese, these are called "san choy bao," or raw vegetable wraps. The lettuce gives a wonderfully fresh and crunchy element to each bite. You can garnish the lettuce cups with chopped peanuts or a sprinkle of fried rice noodles for extra crunch.

¾ pound ground beef

2 teaspoons cornstarch

Kosher salt

Freshly ground black pepper

3 tablespoons vegetable oil, divided

1 tablespoon peeled finely minced ginger

2 garlic cloves, finely minced

1 carrot, peeled and julienned

1 (4-ounce) can diced water chestnuts, drained and rinsed

2 tablespoons hoisin sauce

3 scallions, white and green parts separated, thinly sliced

8 broad iceberg (or Bibb) lettuce leaves, trimmed to neat round cups

1. In a bowl, sprinkle the beef with the cornstarch and a pinch each of salt and pepper. Mix well to combine.
2. Heat a wok over medium-high heat until a bead of water sizzles and evaporates on contact. Pour in 2 tablespoons of oil and swirl to coat the base of the wok. Add the beef and brown on both sides, then toss and flip, breaking up the beef into crumbles and clumps for 3 to 4 minutes, until the beef is no longer pink. Transfer the beef to a clean bowl and set aside.
3. Wipe the wok clean and return it to medium heat. Add the remaining 1 tablespoon of oil and quickly stir-fry the ginger and garlic with a pinch of salt. As soon as the garlic is fragrant, toss in the carrot and water chestnuts for 2 to 3 minutes, until the carrot becomes tender. Lower the heat to medium, return the beef to the wok, and toss with the hoisin sauce and the scallion whites. Toss to combine, about another 45 seconds.
4. Spread out the lettuce leaves, 2 per plate, and evenly divide the beef mixture among the lettuce leaves. Garnish with the scallion greens and eat as you would a soft taco.

SUBSTITUTION TIP: Swap out the ground beef for beef sirloin tips, cut into ½-inch pieces, or use ground pork, ground turkey, or tofu.

Fried Pork Chops with Onion

SERVES 4 ; PREP TIME: 20 MINUTES ; COOK TIME: 15 MINUTES

When he was nine years old, Terri's younger brother Tim asked his mom Alice to teach his future wife how to make these pork chops so that when he married her, he would have them every night for dinner. True, this was a frequent favorite in the Dien household—and now it can be a favorite at yours!

4 boneless pork loin chops

1 tablespoon Shaoxing wine

½ teaspoon freshly ground black pepper

Kosher salt

3 cups vegetable oil

2 tablespoons cornstarch

3 peeled fresh ginger slices, each about the size of a quarter

1 medium yellow onion, thinly sliced

2 garlic cloves, finely minced

2 tablespoons light soy sauce

1 teaspoon dark soy sauce

½ teaspoon red wine vinegar

Sugar

1. Pound the pork chops with a meat mallet until they are ½ inch thick. Place in a bowl and season with the rice wine, pepper, and a small pinch of salt. Marinate for 10 minutes.
2. Pour the oil into the wok; the oil should be about 1 to 1½ inches deep. Bring the oil to 375°F over medium-high heat. You can tell the oil is at the right temperature when you dip the end of a wooden spoon into the oil. If the oil bubbles and sizzles around it, the oil is ready.
3. Working in 2 batches, coat the chops with the cornstarch. Gently lower them one at a time into the oil and fry for 5 to 6 minutes, until golden. Transfer to a paper towel–lined plate.
4. Pour out all but 1 tablespoon of oil from the wok and set it over medium-high heat. Season the oil by adding the ginger and a pinch of salt. Allow the ginger to sizzle in the oil for about 30 seconds, swirling gently.
5. Stir-fry the onion for about 4 minutes, until translucent and soft. Add the garlic and stir-fry for another 30 seconds, or until fragrant. Transfer to the plate with the pork chops.
6. Into the wok, pour the light soy, dark soy, red wine vinegar, and a pinch of sugar and stir to combine. Bring to a boil and return the onion and pork chops to the wok. Toss to

combine as the sauce begins to thicken slightly. Remove the ginger and discard. Transfer to a platter and serve immediately.

SUBSTITUTION TIP: This recipe also works great with chicken cutlets, which might be Terri's favorite over the pork chops.

Five Spice Pork with Bok Choy

SERVES 4 ; PREP TIME: 15 MINUTES ; COOK TIME: 10 MINUTES

Chinese five spice is a blend of spices including cinnamon, cloves, fennel seeds, star anise, and Sichuan peppercorns. We've also made a seven spice blend by adding ground ginger and nutmeg. The spice mix lends a deep, sweet, and aromatic flavor to the pork, but it works great with fish, chicken, or beef.

1 tablespoon light soy sauce

1 tablespoon Shaoxing rice wine

1 teaspoon Chinese five spice powder

1 teaspoon cornstarch

½ teaspoon light brown sugar

¾ pound ground pork

2 tablespoons vegetable oil

2 garlic cloves, peeled and slightly smashed

Kosher salt

2 to 3 heads bok choy, cut crosswise into bite-size pieces

1 carrot, peeled and julienned

Cooked rice, for serving

1. In a mixing bowl, stir together the light soy, rice wine, five spice powder, cornstarch, and brown sugar. Add the pork and mix gently to combine. Set aside to marinate for 10 minutes.
2. Heat a wok over medium-high heat until a drop of water sizzles and evaporates on contact. Pour in the oil and swirl to coat the base of the wok. Season the oil by adding the garlic and a pinch of salt. Allow the garlic to sizzle in the oil for about 10 seconds, swirling gently.
3. Add pork to the wok and leave it to sear against the wok's walls for 1 to 2 minutes, or until a golden crust develops. Flip and sear on the other side for another minute more. Toss and flip to stir-fry the pork for 1 to 2 more minutes, breaking it up into crumbles and clumps until no longer pink.
4. Add the bok choy and carrot and toss and flip to combine with the pork. Keep stir-frying for 2 to 3 minutes, until the carrot and bok choy are tender. Transfer to a platter and serve hot with steamed rice.

Hoisin Pork Stir-Fry

SERVES 4 ; PREP TIME: 15 MINUTES ; COOK TIME: 10 MINUTES

Hoisin sauce might be considered the ketchup of Chinese cooking. It's tasty and easy to use, and can be added to just about any stir-fry recipe that needs a savory-sweet balance. You can vary this dish by adding any sliced vegetables you like. Celery gives a fresh, crunchy texture, but green beans or sliced carrots will do just fine.

2 teaspoons Shaoxing rice wine

2 teaspoons light soy sauce

½ teaspoon chili paste

¾ pound boneless pork loin, thinly sliced into julienne strips

2 tablespoons vegetable oil

4 peeled fresh ginger slices, each about the size of a quarter

Kosher salt

4 ounces snow peas, thinly sliced on the diagonal

2 tablespoons hoisin sauce

1 tablespoon water

1. In a bowl, stir together the rice wine, light soy, and chili paste. Add the pork and toss to coat. Set aside to marinate for 10 minutes.
2. Heat a wok over medium-high heat until a drop of water sizzles and evaporates on contact. Pour in the oil and swirl to coat the base of the wok. Season the oil by adding the ginger and a pinch of salt. Allow the ginger to sizzle in the oil for about 30 seconds, swirling gently.
3. Add the pork and marinade and stir-fry for 2 to 3 minutes, until no longer pink. Add the snow peas and stir-fry for about 1 minute, until tender and translucent. Stir in the hoisin sauce and water to loosen the sauce. Continue to toss and flip for 30 seconds, or until the sauce is heated through and the pork and snow peas are coated.
4. Transfer to a platter and serve hot.

PREP TIP: This is a quick stir-fry to pull together. The trick is to slice the pork into very thin strips so they cook very quickly in the hot wok.

Twice-Cooked Pork Belly

SERVES 4 ; PREP TIME: 10 MINUTES, PLUS OVERNIGHT CHILLING TIME ; COOK TIME: 45 MINUTES

This is one of our favorite make-ahead recipes for entertaining. The pork can be made the day before and finished in the wok just before you serve it. Yes, this recipe takes a little longer, but it's well worth the wait.

1 pound boneless pork belly

⅓ cup Black Bean Sauce or store-bought black bean sauce

1 tablespoon Shaoxing rice wine

1 teaspoon dark soy sauce

½ teaspoon sugar

2 tablespoons vegetable oil, divided

4 peeled fresh ginger slices, each about the size of a quarter

Kosher salt

1 leek, halved lengthwise and cut on the diagonal into ½-inch slices

½ red bell pepper, sliced

1. In a large saucepan, place the pork and cover with water. Bring the pan to a boil and then reduce to a simmer. Simmer uncovered for 30 minutes, or until the pork is tender and cooked through. Using a slotted spoon, transfer the pork to a bowl (discard the cooking liquid) and allow to cool. Refrigerate for several hours or overnight. Once the pork is cool, thinly slice into ¼-inch-thick slices and set aside. Allowing the pork to cool completely before slicing will make it easier to thinly slice.
2. In a glass measuring cup, stir together the black bean sauce, rice wine, dark soy, and sugar and set aside.
3. Heat a wok over medium-high heat until a drop of water sizzles and evaporates on contact. Pour in 1 tablespoon of oil and swirl to coat the base of the wok. Season the oil by adding the ginger and a pinch of salt. Allow the ginger to sizzle in the oil for about 30 seconds, swirling gently.
4. Working in batches, transfer half the pork to the wok. Let the pieces sear in the wok for 2 to 3 minutes. Flip to sear on the other side for another 1 to 2 minutes more, until the pork begins to curl. Transfer to a clean bowl. Repeat with the remaining pork.
5. Add the remaining 1 tablespoon of oil. Add the leek and red pepper and stir-fry for 1 minute, until the leek is soft. Swirl in the sauce and stir-fry until fragrant. Return the pork to the pan and continue stir-frying for 2 to 3 more minutes, until everything is just cooked through. Discard the ginger slices and transfer to a serving platter.

PREP TIP: Leeks collect a lot of dirt. To prevent this dirt from ending up in your dish, wash the leek thoroughly by splitting it lengthwise, leaving the roots on. Fan the leek leaves under running water to remove dirt, making sure to get water in all the layers. Cut off the tough dark green top and save in the freezer for making stock, or discard. Cut the remaining white and light green parts as directed in your recipe and discard the root.

Mu Shu Pork with Skillet Pancakes

SERVES 4 ; PREP TIME: 15 MINUTES, PLUS 30 MINUTES RESTING TIME ; COOK TIME: 20 MINUTES

Nearly every culture has a dish featuring savory filling wrapped in a crêpe, pancake, or tortilla. Our favorite thing about making mu shu pork at home is producing a soft and delicious pancake. Yes, this recipe involves a little more work, but the results are worth the extra effort.

FOR THE PANCAKES

1¾ cups all-purpose flour

¾ cup boiling water

Kosher salt

3 tablespoons sesame oil

FOR THE MU SHU PORK

2 tablespoons light soy sauce

1 teaspoon cornstarch

1 teaspoon Shaoxing rice wine

Ground white pepper

¾ pound boneless pork loin, sliced against the grain into ¼-inch-wide strips

3 tablespoons vegetable oil

2 teaspoons peeled finely minced fresh ginger

Kosher salt

1 large carrot, peeled and thinly julienned to 3-inch lengths

6 to 8 fresh wood ear mushrooms, thinly sliced into julienne strips

½ small head green cabbage, shredded

2 scallions, cut into ½-inch lengths

1 (4-ounce) can sliced bamboo shoots, drained and julienned into thin strips

¼ cup Plum Sauce, for serving

TO MAKE THE PANCAKES

1. In a large mixing bowl, using a wooden spoon, stir together the flour, boiling water, and a pinch of salt. Combine it all until it becomes a shaggy dough. Transfer the dough to a floured cutting board and knead by hand for about 4 minutes, or until smooth. The dough will be hot, so wear disposable gloves to protect your hands. Return the dough to the bowl and cover with plastic wrap. Let rest for 30 minutes.
2. Shape the dough into a 12-inch-long log by rolling it out with your hands. Cut the log into 12 even pieces, keeping the round shape to create medallions. Flatten the medallions with your palms and brush the tops with the sesame oil. Press the oiled sides together, to create 6 stacks of doubled dough pieces.

3. Roll each stack into one thin, round sheet, 7 to 8 inches in diameter. It's best to keep flipping the pancake over as you roll, to achieve an even thinness for both sides.
4. Heat a cast-iron pan over medium-high heat and cook the pancakes one at a time for about 1 minute on the first side, until it turns slightly translucent and begins to blister. Flip to cook the other side, another 30 seconds. Transfer the pancake to a plate lined with a kitchen towel and carefully pull the two pancakes apart. Keep them covered under the towel to stay warm while you carry on with the remaining pancakes. Set aside until ready to serve.

TO MAKE THE MU SHU PORK

5. In a mixing bowl, mix the light soy, cornstarch, rice wine, and a pinch of white pepper. Add the sliced pork and toss to coat and marinate for 10 minutes.
6. Heat a wok over medium-high heat until a drop of water sizzles and evaporates on contact. Pour in the vegetable oil and swirl to coat the base of the wok. Season the oil by adding the ginger and a pinch of salt. Allow the ginger to sizzle in the oil for about 10 seconds, swirling gently.
7. Add the pork and stir-fry 1 to 2 minutes, until no longer pink. Add the carrot and mushrooms and continue to stir-fry for 2 more minutes, or until the carrot is tender. Add the cabbage, scallions, and bamboo shoots and stir-fry for another minute, or until heated through. Transfer to a bowl and serve by spooning the pork filling in the center of a pancake and topping with plum sauce.

SUBSTITUTION TIP: Use thinly shredded chicken instead of pork for Mu Shu Chicken.

Cumin-Spiced Lamb

SERVES 4 ; PREP TIME: 20 MINUTES ; COOK TIME: 15 MINUTES

The Xianjiang region of China sits in the upper northwest corner, and its cuisine benefits from a variety of cultures, including Chinese Muslims and the Uyghurs. Halal lamb is a staple protein served in these communities, which has influenced many lamb dishes in Chinese cuisines throughout the world. Cumin provides the prominent flavor in this dish, so toasting cumin seeds and grinding them yourself can increase the flavor—just one whiff can make you instantly hungry!

¾ pound boneless leg of lamb, cut into 1-inch pieces

1 tablespoon light soy sauce

1 tablespoon Shaoxing rice wine

Kosher salt

2 tablespoons ground cumin

1 teaspoon Sichuan peppercorns, crushed

½ teaspoon sugar

3 tablespoons vegetable oil, divided

4 peeled fresh ginger slices, each about the size of a quarter

2 tablespoons cornstarch

½ yellow onion, sliced lengthwise into strips

6 to 8 whole dried Chinese chili peppers (optional)

4 garlic cloves, thinly sliced

½ bunch fresh cilantro, coarsely chopped

1. In a mixing bowl, combine the lamb, light soy, rice wine, and a small pinch of salt. Toss to coat and marinate for 15 minutes, or overnight in the refrigerator.
2. In another bowl, stir together the cumin, Sichuan peppercorns, and sugar. Set aside.
3. Heat a wok over medium-high heat until a drop of water sizzles and evaporates on contact. Pour in 2 tablespoons of oil and swirl to coat the base of the wok. Season the oil by adding the ginger and a pinch of salt. Allow the ginger to sizzle in the oil for about 30 seconds, swirling gently.
4. Toss the lamb pieces with the cornstarch and add to the hot wok. Sear the lamb for 2 to 3 minutes per side, and then stir-fry for 1 or 2 minutes more, tossing and flipping around the wok. Transfer the lamb to a clean bowl and set aside.
5. Add the remaining 1 tablespoon of oil and swirl to coat the wok. Toss in the onion and chili peppers (if using) and stir-fry for 3 to 4 minutes, or until the onion begins to look shiny but not limp. Season lightly with a small pinch of salt. Toss in the garlic and spice mixture and continue to stir-fry for another minute.

6. Return the lamb to the wok and toss to combine for 1 to 2 minutes more. Transfer to a platter, discard the ginger, and garnish with the cilantro.

PREP TIP: The lamb should be seared on the outside but medium-rare on the inside. If you prefer medium, cook for 1 to 2 minutes longer.

Pork Spareribs with Black Bean Sauce

SERVES 4 ; PREP TIME: 15 MINUTES ; COOK TIME: 20 MINUTES

Pai gwut, as it is known in Cantonese, are little bite-size morsels of succulent pork ribs punctuated with salty black beans, and a staple at many dim sum restaurants. The spareribs are cut into 1½-inch lengths, then separated so they are small enough to pop into your mouth. Buy baby back ribs from a butcher who can cut these down for you with a bandsaw.

1 pound pork spareribs, cut crosswise into 1½-inch-wide strips

¼ teaspoon ground white pepper

2 tablespoons Black Bean Sauce or store-bought black bean sauce

1 tablespoon Shaoxing rice wine

1 tablespoon vegetable oil

2 teaspoons cornstarch

½-inch fresh ginger piece, peeled and finely minced

2 garlic cloves, finely minced

1 teaspoon sesame oil

2 scallions, thinly sliced

1. Slice between the ribs to separate them into bite-size riblets. In a shallow, heatproof bowl, combine the ribs and white pepper. Add the black bean sauce, rice wine, vegetable oil, cornstarch, ginger, and garlic and toss to combine, making sure the riblets are all coated. Marinate for 10 minutes.
2. Rinse a bamboo steamer basket and its lid under cold water and place it in the wok. Pour in 2 inches of water, or until it comes above the bottom rim of the steamer by about ¼ to ½ inch, but not so much that it touches the bottom of the basket. Place the bowl with the ribs in the steamer basket and cover.
3. Turn the heat to high to boil the water, then lower the heat to medium-high. Steam over medium-high heat for 20 to 22 minutes, or until the riblets are no longer pink. You may need to replenish the water, so keep checking to make sure it doesn't boil dry in the wok.
4. Remove the bowl carefully from the steamer basket. Drizzle the ribs with the sesame oil and garnish with the scallions. Serve immediately.

Stir-Fried Mongolian Lamb

SERVES 4 ; PREP TIME: 15 MINUTES ; COOK TIME: 15 MINUTES

Like Mongolian beef, this dish didn't originate in Mongolia. Chilies are optional in this simple stir-fried lamb dish, but don't skimp on them if you like spice.

2 tablespoons Shaoxing rice wine

1 tablespoon dark soy sauce

3 garlic cloves, minced

2 teaspoons cornstarch

1 teaspoon sesame oil

1 pound boneless leg of lamb, cut into ¼-inch-thick slices

3 tablespoons vegetable oil, divided

4 peeled fresh ginger slices, each about the size of a quarter

2 whole dried red chili peppers (optional)

Kosher salt

4 scallions, cut into 3-inch-long pieces, then thinly sliced lengthwise

1. In a large bowl, stir together the rice wine, dark soy, garlic, cornstarch, and sesame oil. Add the lamb to the marinade and toss to coat. Marinate for 10 minutes.
2. Heat a wok over medium-high heat until a drop of water sizzles and evaporates on contact. Pour in 2 tablespoons of vegetable oil and swirl to coat the base of the wok. Season the oil by adding the ginger, chilies (if using), and a pinch of salt. Allow the aromatics to sizzle in the oil for about 30 seconds, swirling gently.
3. Using tongs, lift half the lamb from the marinade, shaking slightly to let the excess drip off. Reserve the marinade. Sear in the wok for 2 to 3 minutes. Flip to sear on the other side for another 1 to 2 minutes. Stir-fry by tossing and flipping around in the wok quickly for 1 more minute. Transfer to a clean bowl. Add the remaining 1 tablespoon of vegetable oil and repeat with the remaining lamb.
4. Return all of the lamb and the reserved marinade to the wok and toss in the scallions. Stir-fry for another 1 minute, or until the lamb is cooked through and the marinade turns into a shiny sauce.
5. Transfer to a serving platter, discard the ginger, and serve hot.

Lamb with Ginger and Leeks

SERVES 4 ; PREP TIME: 10 MINUTES ; COOK TIME: 15 MINUTES

Lamb is served mainly within the inland regions of China, and is rarely seen in the coastal provinces, like Shanghai. If you find the taste of lamb too gamey, marinate it in Shaoxing rice wine to mellow it out quite a bit. We like the pairing of lamb with mild and bright green leeks—it feels Continental, yet Chinese at the same time.

¾ pound boneless leg of lamb, cut into 3 chunks, then thinly sliced across the grain

Kosher salt

2 tablespoons Shaoxing rice wine

1 tablespoon dark soy sauce

1 tablespoon light soy sauce

1 teaspoon oyster sauce

1 teaspoon honey

1 to 2 teaspoons sesame oil

½ teaspoon ground Sichuan pepper corns

2 teaspoons cornstarch

2 tablespoons vegetable oil

1 tablespoon peeled and finely minced fresh ginger

2 leeks, trimmed and thinly sliced

4 garlic cloves, finely minced

1. In a mixing bowl, season the lamb lightly with 1 to 2 pinches of salt. Toss to coat and set aside for 10 minutes. In a small bowl, stir together the rice wine, dark soy, light soy, oyster sauce, honey, sesame oil, Sichuan pepper, and cornstarch. Set aside.
2. Heat a wok over medium-high heat until a drop of water sizzles and evaporates on contact. Pour in the vegetable oil and swirl to coat the base of the wok. Season the oil by adding the ginger and a pinch of salt. Allow the ginger to sizzle in the oil for about 10 seconds, swirling gently.
3. Add the lamb and sear for 1 to 2 minutes, then begin to stir-fry, tossing and flipping for 2 minutes more, or until no longer pink. Transfer to a clean bowl and set aside.
4. Add the leeks and garlic and stir-fry for 1 to 2 minutes, or until the leeks are bright green and soft. Transfer to the lamb bowl.
5. Pour in the sauce mixture and simmer for 3 to 4 minutes, until the sauce reduces by half and turns glossy. Return the lamb and vegetables to the wok and toss to combine with the sauce.
6. Transfer to a platter and serve hot.

PREP TIP: Don't have a spice grinder or mortar and pestle to grind your peppercorns? Not to worry. You can grind spices by smashing them between a cutting board and the bottom of a heavy skillet. Hold the sides of the skillet like a steering wheel and press down on the cutting board, grinding in tight circular motions to grind the spices.

SOUPS, RICE, AND NOODLES

Sizzling Rice Soup

SERVES 4 ; PREP TIME: 20 MINUTES ; COOK TIME: 15 MINUTES

"Fun" is the best way to describe this soup. The snap, crackle, and pop experience of this light, brothy soup with a pile of sizzling, crispy fried rice floating in the middle like Pop Rocks offers a toasty flavor to the otherwise clean, simple soup. The extra step of preparing the rice to get the right sizzling effect is worth it.

1 cup cooked rice

4 cups low-sodium chicken broth

4 fresh shiitake mushrooms, stems removed and caps thinly sliced

1 large carrot, peeled and cut into ¼-inch-thick slices

2 teaspoons light soy sauce

2 teaspoons sesame oil

1 teaspoon Shaoxing rice wine

2 baby bok choy heads, chopped into bite-size pieces

10 to 12 medium shrimp (U41–50), peeled and deveined

3 cups vegetable oil

1. Preheat the oven to 300°F. Line a baking sheet with parchment paper or aluminum foil. Spread the rice in an even layer and bake for 15 to 20 minutes, until it feels dry. Set aside to cool.
2. In a soup pot, bring the chicken broth to a boil over high heat. Lower the heat to medium-high and add the mushrooms and carrot. Add the light soy, sesame oil, and rice wine to the soup and simmer for 5 minutes.
3. Add the bok choy and bring to a boil over high heat. Turn the heat down to simmer and add the shrimp. Stir to distribute the vegetables and shrimp and simmer over low heat while you fry the rice.
4. Pour the oil into the wok; the oil should be about 1 to 1½ inches deep. Bring the oil to 375°F over medium-high heat. You can tell the oil is at the right temperature by dipping the end of a wooden spoon into the oil. If the oil bubbles and sizzles around it, the oil is ready.
5. Fry the rice a scoopful at a time, until golden brown and crispy, 2 to 3 minutes. Use a wire skimmer to lift the rice in clumps out of the oil and transfer to a paper towel–lined plate.
6. When ready to serve, divide the soup and vegetables among 4 soup bowls. Top each bowl with the crispy rice and serve while still sizzling.

PREP TIP: This is a great way to use up leftover cooked rice. Bake it off and keep it in an airtight container, then fry it just before serving the soup.

Pork Congee

SERVES 4 ; PREP TIME: 20 MINUTES ; COOK TIME: 90 MINUTES

We eat congee when we feel under the weather, and it soothes us when we are tired or brokenhearted . . . it's the Chinese equivalent of chicken noodle soup. It cures all! Amp up the flavor by making the congee with a mix of water and low-sodium chicken broth.

10 cups water

¾ cup jasmine rice, rinsed and drained

1 teaspoon kosher salt

2 teaspoons peeled minced fresh ginger

2 garlic cloves, minced

1 tablespoon light soy sauce, plus more for serving

2 teaspoons Shaoxing rice wine

2 teaspoons cornstarch

6 ounces ground pork

2 tablespoons vegetable oil

Pickled Chinese vegetables, thinly sliced, for serving (optional)

Scallion-Ginger Oil, for serving (optional)

Fried Chili Oil, for serving (optional)

Sesame oil, for serving (optional)

1. In a heavy-bottomed pot, bring the water to a boil. Stir in the rice and salt and reduce the heat to a simmer. Cover and cook, stirring occasionally, for about 1½ hours, until the rice has turned to a soft porridge-like consistency.
2. While the congee is cooking, in a medium bowl, stir together the ginger, garlic, light soy, rice wine, and cornstarch. Add the pork and allow it to marinate for 15 minutes.
3. Heat a wok over medium-high heat until a drop of water sizzles and evaporates on contact. Pour in the vegetable oil and swirl to coat the base of the wok. Add the pork and stir-fry, tossing and breaking up the meat, about 2 minutes. Cook for another 1 to 2 minutes without stirring to get some caramelization.
4. Serve the congee in soup bowls topped with the stir-fried pork. Garnish with your toppings of choice.

Egg Fried Rice (Chao Fan)

SERVES 4 ; PREP TIME: 20 minutes ; COOK TIME: 5 minutes

This recipe, also called chao fan, is the most basic fried rice across all of Asia. When making fried rice, always use leftover rice. Trying to stir-fry freshly cooked rice will result in a mess of overcooked mushy rice. Letting the rice cool and dry overnight or in a flat pan for at least several hours will result in perfect fried rice. Master this recipe and all the other fried rice recipes are yours for the making.

2 tablespoons cooking oil

2 garlic cloves, crushed and chopped

1 tablespoon crushed and chopped ginger

4 large eggs, scrambled

4 scallions, cut diagonally into ¼-inch pieces

2 cups cooked day-old rice

½ teaspoon salt

½ teaspoon black or white pepper

1 tablespoon soy sauce

1 teaspoon toasted sesame oil

1. In a wok, heat the cooking oil over high heat until it begins to smoke.
2. Add the garlic, ginger, and eggs to the wok and stir-fry for 2 minutes, or until the eggs are cooked.
3. Add the scallions, rice, salt, pepper, soy sauce, and sesame oil and stir-fry for 1 minute, or until all the ingredients are well combined, then serve.

INGREDIENT TIP: Short- or medium-grain rice, such as a Japanese sushi variety, makes fried rice that is softer and stickier than fried rice made from a long-grain rice such as jasmine or basmati.

Fried Rice with Shrimp, Egg, and Scallions

SERVES 4 ; PREP TIME: 10 MINUTES ; COOK TIME: 10 MINUTES

Fried rice seems so simple, and it is, for sure. There are just a couple of things to know in order to make the great fried rice at home. First, using day-old rice is the only way to get the right texture. Freshly cooked rice will result in mushy fried rice. Keep a bag of cooked rice in the freezer for when the mood for fried rice strikes. And the second thing is actually a secret: butter. Fried rice is infinitely better with butter!

2 tablespoons vegetable oil

Kosher salt

1 large egg, beaten

½ pound shrimp (any size), peeled, deveined, and cut into bite-size pieces

1 teaspoon peeled finely minced fresh ginger

2 garlic cloves, finely minced

½ cup frozen peas and carrots

2 scallions, thinly sliced, divided

3 cups cold cooked rice

3 tablespoons unsalted butter

1 tablespoon light soy sauce

1 tablespoon sesame oil

1. Heat a wok over medium-high heat until a drop of water sizzles and evaporates on contact. Pour in the vegetable oil and swirl to coat the base of the wok. Season the oil by adding a small pinch of salt. Add the egg and scramble quickly.
2. Push the egg to the sides of the wok to create a center ring and add the shrimp, ginger, and garlic together. Stir-fry the shrimp with a small pinch of salt for 2 to 3 minutes, until they turn opaque and pink. Add the peas and carrots and half the scallions and stir-fry for another minute.
3. Add the rice, breaking up any large lumps, and toss and flip to combine all of the ingredients. Stir-fry for 1 minute, then push it all to the sides of the wok, leaving a well in the bottom of the wok.
4. Add the butter and light soy, let the butter melt and bubble, then toss everything together to coat, about 30 seconds.
5. Spread the fried rice in an even layer in the wok and let the rice sit against the wok for about 2 minutes to crisp up slightly. Drizzle with the sesame oil and season with another small pinch of salt. Transfer to a platter and serve immediately, garnishing with the rest of the scallions.

SUBSTITUTION TIP: Fried rice is the best thing ever to have happened to leftovers and scraps of vegetables, so use whatever you have on hand. We like using sliced broccoli stems and leftover cooked proteins like pork, chicken, and beef.

Egg Drop Soup

SERVES 4 ; PREP TIME: 5 MINUTES ; COOK TIME: 10 MINUTES

This soup is ubiquitous on Chinese restaurant menus. The savory soup is comforting, and the delicate ribbons of egg make it look really special. Why order out, when you can make it with what you have in your pantry and refrigerator in just a few minutes?

4 cups low-sodium chicken broth

2 peeled fresh ginger slices, each about the size of a quarter

2 garlic cloves, peeled

2 teaspoons light soy sauce

2 tablespoons cornstarch

3 tablespoons water

2 large eggs, lightly beaten

1 teaspoon sesame oil

2 scallions, thinly sliced, for garnish

1. In a wok or soup pot, combine the broth, ginger, garlic, and light soy and bring to a boil. Reduce to a simmer and cook for 5 minutes. Remove and discard the ginger and garlic.
2. In a small bowl, mix the cornstarch and water and stir the mixture into the wok. Return the heat to medium-high and stir for about 30 seconds, until the soup thickens.
3. Reduce the heat to a simmer. Dip a fork into the beaten eggs and then drag it through the soup, gently stirring as you go. Continue to dip the fork into the egg and drag it through the soup to create the egg threads. When all the egg has been added, simmer the soup undisturbed for a few moments to set the eggs. Stir in the sesame oil and ladle the soup into serving bowls. Garnish with the scallions.

VARIATION TIP: Add a couple handfuls of your favorite greens or leftover rice before adding the eggs. Defrosted corn kernels, peas, and shrimp? These additions may not be traditional, but they round out the soup to make it a meal.

Hot-and-Sour Soup

SERVES 4 ; PREP TIME: 20 MINUTES ; COOK TIME: 15 MINUTES

China has long understood the concept of "food as medicine." The hot and sour flavors of the soup help balance the yin and yang of the body, bringing it back into balance. Hot-and-sour soup is low in calories, dense with vitamins and nutrients, warming and soothing for an upset stomach, and calming and clearing for the respiratory system, making it a delicious tonic for everyday meals or when your body just feels a little out of whack.

4 ounces boneless pork loin, cut into ¼-inch-thick strips

1 tablespoon dark soy sauce

4 dried shiitake mushrooms

8 dried tree ear mushrooms

1½ tablespoons cornstarch

¼ cup unseasoned rice vinegar

2 tablespoons light soy sauce

2 teaspoons sugar

1 teaspoon Fried Chili Oil

1 teaspoon ground white pepper

2 tablespoons vegetable oil

1 peeled fresh ginger slice, about the size of a quarter

Kosher salt

4 cups low-sodium chicken broth

4 ounces firm tofu, rinsed and cut into ¼-inch strips

1 large egg, lightly beaten

2 scallions, thinly sliced, for garnish

1. In a bowl, toss the pork and dark soy to coat. Set aside.
2. Place both mushrooms in a heatproof bowl and cover with boiling water. Soak the mushrooms until softened, about 20 minutes. Pour off ¼ cup of the mushroom water into a glass measuring cup and set aside. Drain and discard the rest of the liquid. Thinly slice the shiitake mushrooms and cut the tree ear mushrooms into bite-size pieces. Return both mushrooms to the soaking bowl and set aside.
3. Stir the cornstarch into the reserved mushroom liquid until the cornstarch has dissolved. Stir in the vinegar, light soy, sugar, chili oil, and white pepper until the sugar has dissolved. Set aside.
4. Heat a wok over medium-high heat until a drop of water sizzles and evaporates on contact. Pour in the vegetable oil and swirl to coat the base of the wok. Season the oil by

adding the ginger and a pinch of salt. Allow the ginger to sizzle in the oil for about 30 seconds, swirling gently.

5. Transfer the pork to the wok and stir-fry for about 3 minutes, until the pork is no longer pink. Remove the ginger and discard. Add the broth and bring to a boil. Reduce to a simmer and stir in the mushrooms. Simmer the mushrooms for about 2 minutes. Stir in the tofu and simmer for 2 minutes. Stir in the cornstarch mixture and return the heat to medium-high, stirring until the soup thickens, about 30 seconds. Reduce the heat to a simmer.
6. Dip a fork into the beaten egg and then drag it through the soup, gently stirring as you go. Continue to dip the fork into the egg and drag it through the soup to create the egg threads. When all of the egg has been added, simmer the soup undisturbed for a few moments to set the egg threads. Ladle the soup into serving bowls and garnish with the scallions.

PREP TIP: Make the soup ahead of time but leave out the egg. Heat the soup in a saucepan and add the egg just before serving.

Smoked Trout Fried Rice

SERVES 4 ; PREP TIME: 10 MINUTES ; COOK TIME: 10 MINUTES

This fusion dish was inspired by another traditional homestyle comfort food: hahm yue chow fan, or salted fish fried rice. Mia likes to use ghee, or clarified butter, to make it even richer.

2 large eggs

1 teaspoon sesame oil

Kosher salt

Ground white pepper

1 tablespoon light soy sauce

½ teaspoon sugar

3 tablespoons ghee or vegetable oil, divided

1 teaspoon peeled finely minced fresh ginger

2 garlic cloves, finely minced

3 cups cold cooked rice

4 ounces smoked trout, broken into bite-size pieces

½ cup thinly sliced hearts of romaine lettuce

2 scallions, thinly sliced

½ teaspoon white sesame seeds

1. In a large bowl, whisk the eggs with the sesame oil and a pinch each of salt and white pepper until just combined. In a small bowl, stir the light soy and sugar together to dissolve the sugar. Set aside.
2. Heat a wok over medium-high heat until a drop of water sizzles and evaporates on contact. Pour in 1 tablespoon of ghee and swirl to coat the base of the wok. Add the egg mixture and, using a heatproof spatula, swirl and shake the eggs to cook. Transfer the eggs to a plate when just cooked but not dry.
3. Add the remaining 2 tablespoons of ghee to the wok, along with the ginger and garlic. Stir-fry quickly until the garlic and ginger just become aromatic, but take care not to let them burn. Add the rice and soy mixture and stir to combine. Continue stir-frying, about 3 minutes. Add the trout and cooked egg and stir-fry to break them up, about 20 seconds. Add the lettuce and scallions and stir-fry until they are both bright green.
4. Transfer to a serving platter and sprinkle with the sesame seeds.

Spam Fried Rice

SERVES 4 ; PREP TIME: 5 MINUTES ; COOK TIME: 15 MINUTES

If you are a fan of pizza with ham and pineapple on it, then this one's for you! The balance of the sweet pineapple with the savory Spam is addicting. Yet again, this recipe highlights a quick and easy pantry meal, as well as the influence of Chinese food from Hawaii. Garnish with chopped honey-roasted peanuts, which is Terri's favorite.

1 tablespoon vegetable oil

2 peeled fresh ginger slices, each about the size of a quarter

Kosher salt

1 (12-ounce) can Spam, cut into ½-inch cubes

½ white onion, cut to ¼-inch cubes

2 garlic cloves, finely minced

½ cup frozen peas and carrots

2 scallions, thinly sliced, divided

3 cups cold cooked rice

½ cup canned pineapple chunks, juices reserved

3 tablespoons unsalted butter

2 tablespoons light soy sauce

1 teaspoon sriracha

1 teaspoon light brown sugar

1 tablespoon sesame oil

1. Heat a wok over medium-high heat until a drop of water sizzles and evaporates on contact. Pour in the vegetable oil and swirl to coat the base of the wok. Season the oil by adding the ginger and a small pinch of salt. Allow the ginger to sizzle in the oil for about 30 seconds, swirling gently.
2. Add the diced Spam and spread it out evenly across the bottom of the wok. Let the Spam sear before tossing and flipping. Continue to stir-fry the Spam for 5 to 6 minutes, until it turns golden and crispy around all sides.
3. Add the onion and garlic and stir-fry for about 2 minutes, until the onion begins to look translucent. Add the peas and carrots and half the scallions. Stir-fry for another minute more.
4. Toss in the rice and pineapple, breaking up any large clumps of rice, and toss and flip to combine all of the ingredients. Stir-fry for 1 minute, then push it all to the sides of the wok, leaving a well in the bottom of the wok.

5. Add the butter, reserved pineapple juice, light soy, sriracha, and brown sugar. Stir to dissolve the sugar and bring the sauce to a boil, then cook for about a minute to reduce the sauce and thicken it slightly. Combine everything to coat, about 30 seconds.
6. Spread the fried rice in an even layer in the wok and let the rice sit against the wok to crisp up slightly, about 2 minutes. Remove the ginger and discard. Drizzle with the sesame oil and season with another small pinch of salt. Transfer to a platter and garnish with the remaining scallions. Serve immediately.

PREP TIP: Keep a bag of cooked rice in the freezer for when the mood for fried rice strikes.

Steamed Rice with Lap Cheung and Bok Choy

SERVES 4 ; PREP TIME: 2 HOURS ; COOK TIME: 20 MINUTES

This dish is normally made in a rice cooker, but we wanted to show you how steaming rice in a steamer basket can work, too. Lap cheung, or Chinese sausage, is a rich, smoky, sweet, and savory protein. The fat melts and flavors the rice as it cooks.

1½ cups jasmine rice

4 lap cheung (Chinese sausage) links or Spanish chorizo

4 baby bok choy heads, each sliced into 6 wedges

¼ cup vegetable oil

1 small shallot, thinly sliced

1-inch fresh ginger piece, peeled and finely minced

1 garlic clove, peeled and finely minced

2 teaspoons light soy sauce

1 tablespoon dark soy sauce

2 teaspoons Shaoxing rice wine

1 teaspoon sesame oil

Sugar

1. In a mixing bowl, rinse and swish the rice 3 or 4 times under cold water, swishing the rice around in the water to rinse off any starches. Cover the rice with cold water and soak for 2 hours. Drain the rice through a fine-mesh sieve.
2. Rinse two bamboo steamer baskets and their lids under cold water and place one basket in the wok. Pour in 2 inches of water, or enough to make the water level come above the bottom rim of the steamer by ¼ to ½ inch but not so high that the water touches the bottom of the steamer.
3. Line a plate with a piece of cheesecloth and add half the soaked rice to the plate. Arrange 2 sausages and half the bok choy on top, and loosely tie up the cheesecloth so there is enough space around the rice so that it can expand. Place the plate in the steamer basket. Repeat the process with another plate, more cheesecloth, and the remaining sausage and bok choy in the second steamer basket, then stack it on top of the first and cover.
4. Turn the heat to medium-high and bring the water to a boil. Steam the rice for 20 minutes, checking the water level often and adding more as needed.
5. While the rice is steaming, in a small saucepan, heat the vegetable oil over medium heat until it just begins to smoke. Turn off the heat and add the shallot, ginger, and garlic. Stir together and add the light soy, dark soy, rice wine, sesame oil, and a pinch of sugar. Set aside to cool.

6. When the rice is ready, carefully untie the cheesecloth and transfer the rice and bok choy to a platter. Slice the sausages diagonally and arrange on top of the rice. Serve with the ginger soy oil on the side.

PREP TIP: To save yourself some time, soak the rice overnight in the refrigerator.

Chicken Pad Thai

SERVES 4 ; PREP TIME: 20 MINUTES ; COOK TIME: 5 MINUTES

Invented in the 1930s by the prime minister of Thailand to be the country's national dish, pad Thai has consistently been rated among the top 10 noodle dishes in the world. Its name literally means "Thai stir-fry," and it's the perfect dish to make at home. You can find pad Thai sauce in the international section of most grocery stores, in Asian markets, and online.

8 ounces dried rice noodles

2 quarts water

2 tablespoons cooking oil

1 tablespoon crushed and chopped ginger

2 garlic cloves, crushed and chopped

2 large eggs, beaten

1 pound boneless chicken thighs, cut into 1-inch pieces across the grain

2 bird's eye peppers, cut into ¼-inch pieces

¼ cup pad Thai sauce

½ cup chopped peanuts

1 cup bean sprouts

½ cup coarsely chopped cilantro

1 lime, cut into wedges

1. Prepare the dried rice noodles by bringing the water to a boil and then turning the heat off. Place the noodles in the pot and stir for 1 minute, until the noodles are flexible. Let the noodles soak for 2 to 3 minutes, until the noodles are al dente, cooked but firm. Drain and set them aside.
2. In a wok, heat the cooking oil over high heat until it shimmers.
3. Add the ginger, garlic, and eggs to the wok and stir-fry for 1 minute.
4. Add the chicken and peppers and stir-fry for 1 minute.
5. Add the pad Thai sauce and stir-fry for 1 minute.
6. Serve over the cooked rice noodles and garnish with the chopped peanuts, sprouts, cilantro, and lime wedges.

VARIATION TIP: You can substitute different proteins in pad Thai, such as beef, pork, and other meats. You can also try different garnishes, such as crushed cashews or almonds in place of peanuts.

Garlic Noodles

SERVES 4 ; PREP TIME: 10 MINUTES ; COOK TIME: 10 MINUTES

Garlic noodles normally accompany stir-fried or braised seafood dishes. This is a Chinese twist on the classic American dish made from spaghetti, butter, and garlic.

½ pound fresh Chinese egg noodles

2 tablespoons sesame oil, divided

2 tablespoons light brown sugar

2 tablespoons oyster sauce

1 tablespoon light soy sauce

½ teaspoons ground white pepper

6 tablespoons unsalted butter

8 garlic cloves, finely minced

6 scallions, thinly sliced

1. Bring a pot of water to a boil and cook the noodles according to package directions. Reserve 1 cup of the cooking water, then drain. Drizzle the noodles with 1 tablespoon of sesame oil and toss to coat. Set aside.
2. In a small bowl, stir together the brown sugar, oyster sauce, light soy, and white pepper. Set aside.
3. Heat a wok over medium-high heat and melt the butter until the foaming stops. Add the garlic and half the scallions. Stir-fry for 30 seconds, or until the garlic is softened.
4. Pour in the sauce and stir to combine with the butter and garlic. Bring the sauce to a simmer and add the noodles. Toss the noodles to coat with sauce. If the noodles need to loosen up a bit, add some of the cooking water, 1 tablespoon at a time. Continue to stir-fry the noodles for 2 to 3 minutes, until they are heated through.
5. Transfer the garlic noodles to a platter and garnish with the remaining scallions. Serve hot.

VARIATION TIP: To make Crabby Garlic Noodles, toss ½ pound lump crabmeat (from a can is fine) with the butter and garlic.

Singapore Noodles

SERVES 4 ; PREP TIME: 10 MINUTES ; COOK TIME: 20 MINUTES

No one knows for sure why this delicious dish is called Singapore noodles; it's highly doubtful that the recipe originated in Singapore. One thing is for sure, however: The movement of Chinese around the world has resulted in many classic dishes, including this one. We consider this to be a pantry recipe, with the majority of ingredients coming from your freezer or cupboards. If you like spice, add sriracha, hot chili sauce, or chili oil to serve.

½ pound dried rice vermicelli noodles

½ pound medium shrimp (U41–50), peeled and deveined

1 teaspoon fish sauce (optional)

3 tablespoons coconut oil, divided

Kosher salt

1 small white onion, thinly sliced into strips

½ green bell pepper, cut into thin strips

½ red bell pepper, cut into thin strips

2 garlic cloves, finely minced

1 cup frozen peas, thawed

½ pound char shiu (Chinese roast pork), sliced into thin strips

2 teaspoons curry powder

Freshly ground black pepper

Juice of 1 lime

8 to 10 fresh cilantro sprigs

1. Bring a large pot of water to boil over high heat. Turn off the heat and add the noodles. Soak for 4 to 5 minutes, until the noodles are opaque. Carefully drain the noodles in a colander. Rinse the noodles with cold water and set aside.
2. In a small bowl, season the shrimp with the fish sauce (if using) and set aside for 5 minutes. If you don't wish to use fish sauce, use a pinch of salt to season the shrimp instead.
3. Heat a wok over medium-high heat until a drop of water sizzles and evaporates on contact. Pour in 2 tablespoons of coconut oil and swirl to coat the base of the wok. Season the oil by adding a small pinch of salt. Add the shrimp and stir-fry for 3 to 4 minutes, or until the shrimp turn pink. Transfer to a clean bowl and set aside.
4. Add the remaining 1 tablespoon of coconut oil and swirl to coat the wok. Stir-fry the onion, bell peppers, and garlic for 3 to 4 minutes, until the onions and peppers are soft. Add the peas and stir-fry until just heated through, about another minute.

5. Add the pork and return the shrimp to the wok. Toss together with the curry powder and season with salt and pepper. Add the noodles and toss to combine. The noodles will turn a brilliant golden yellow color as you continue to gently toss them with the other ingredients. Continue stir-frying and tossing for about 2 minutes, until the noodles are heated through.
6. Transfer the noodles to a platter, drizzle with the lime juice, and garnish with the cilantro. Serve immediately.

INGREDIENT TIP: Char shiu, also known as barbecue pork, can be purchased at any Chinese restaurant or market. If you aren't able to get char shiu, any roasted pork will be an acceptable substitute.

Glass Noodles with Green Beans and Napa Cabbage

SERVES 4 ; PREP TIME: 15 MINUTES ; COOK TIME: 10 MINUTES

Searching for a unique side dish to serve with vegetables? Tired of the same noodles and fried rice? Then take this recipe for a spin! When cooked, Asian noodles made from potato starch or mung bean flour turn brilliantly transparent, which is why they are called glass noodles. They can create a visually stunning presentation and have a wonderfully chewy texture. Give these a try—it's so simple to make them.

½ pound dried sweet potato noodles or mung bean noodles

2 tablespoons light soy sauce

2 teaspoons dark soy sauce

1 tablespoon oyster sauce

1 teaspoon sugar

2 tablespoons vegetable oil

2 peeled fresh ginger slices, each about the size of a quarter

Kosher salt

1 teaspoon Sichuan peppercorns

1 small head napa cabbage, chopped into bite-size pieces

½ pound green beans, trimmed and halved

3 scallions, coarsely chopped

1. In a large bowl, soften the noodles by soaking them in hot water for 10 minutes, or until softened. Carefully drain the noodles in a colander. Rinse with cold water and set aside.
2. In a small bowl, mix together the light soy, dark soy, oyster sauce, and sugar. Set aside.
3. Heat a wok over medium-high heat until a drop of water sizzles and evaporates on contact. Pour in the oil and swirl to coat the base of the wok. Season the oil by adding the ginger, a small pinch of salt, and the Sichuan peppercorns. Allow the ginger to sizzle in the oil for about 30 seconds, swirling gently. Scoop out the ginger and peppercorns and discard.
4. Add the napa cabbage and green beans to the wok and stir-fry, tossing and flipping for 3 to 4 minutes, until the vegetables are wilted. Pour in the sauce and toss to combine.
5. Add the noodles and toss to combine with the sauce and vegetables. Cover and lower the heat to medium. Cook for 2 to 3 minutes, or until the noodles turn transparent and the green beans are tender.

6.Increase the heat to medium-high and uncover the wok. Stir-fry, tossing and scooping for another 1 to 2 minutes, until the sauce thickens slightly. Transfer to a platter and garnish with the scallions. Serve hot.

SUBSTITUTION TIP: Switch up the vegetables and use carrots and mushrooms instead, or spinach and red bell peppers. There is no limit to the combination of vegetables in this dish.

Hakka Noodles

SERVES 4 ; PREP TIME: 15 MINUTES ; COOK TIME: 15 MINUTES

Indo-Chinese food, or Hakka cuisine, is popular street food in India, further illustrating how the Chinese diaspora influences regional Chinese food around the world. This is a simple, flexible recipe, using any flour-based noodles (even dried spaghetti) and vegetables you have available. Keep it on the spicier side to make it more satisfying.

¾ pound fresh flour-based noodles

3 tablespoons sesame oil, divided

2 tablespoons light soy sauce

1 tablespoon rice vinegar

2 teaspoons light brown sugar

1 teaspoon sriracha

1 teaspoon Fried Chili Oil

Kosher salt

Ground white pepper

2 tablespoons vegetable oil

1 tablespoon peeled finely minced fresh ginger

½ head green cabbage, shredded

½ red bell pepper, sliced into thin strips

½ red onion, sliced into thin vertical strips

1 large carrot, peeled and julienned

2 garlic cloves, finely minced

4 scallions, thinly sliced

1. Bring a pot of water to a boil and cook the noodles according to package instructions. Drain, rinse, and toss with 2 tablespoons of sesame oil. Set aside.
2. In a small bowl, stir together the light soy, rice vinegar, brown sugar, sriracha, chili oil, and a pinch each of salt and white pepper. Set aside.
3. Heat a wok over medium-high heat until a drop of water sizzles and evaporates on contact. Pour in the vegetable oil and swirl to coat the base of the wok. Season the oil by adding the ginger and a small pinch of salt. Allow the ginger to sizzle in the oil for about 10 seconds, swirling gently.
4. Add the cabbage, bell pepper, onion, and carrot and stir-fry for 4 to 5 minutes, or until the vegetables are tender and the onion begins to caramelize slightly. Add the garlic and stir-fry until fragrant, about 30 seconds more. Stir in the sauce mixture and bring to a

boil. Turn the heat down to medium and simmer the sauce for 1 to 2 minutes. Add the scallions and toss to combine.

5. Add the noodles and toss to combine. Increase the heat to medium-high and stir-fry for 1 to 2 minutes to heat the noodles. Transfer to a platter, drizzle with the remaining 1 tablespoon of sesame oil, and serve hot.

PREP TIP: In a hurry to get dinner on the table? Buy bags of pre-prepped raw vegetables like sliced mushrooms, bell peppers, carrots, peas, and celery. This way, all you have to do is mix the sauce and cook the noodles.

Pad See Ew

SERVES 4 ; PREP TIME: 20 MINUTES ; COOK TIME: 10 MINUTES

Pad see ew is a Thai recipe, but its origins come from Chinese cuisine, as most Asian noodle dishes do. Every Asian culture has its own soy sauce: Thai soy sauce is darker and saltier than Chinese soy sauce, so we are using dark Chinese soy with some extra salt added to approximate the right flavor.

2 teaspoons dark soy sauce

2 teaspoons cornstarch

2 teaspoons fish sauce, divided

½ teaspoon kosher salt

Ground white pepper

¾ pound flank steak or sirloin tips, sliced across the grain into ⅛-inch-thick slices

2 tablespoons oyster sauce

1 tablespoon light soy sauce

½ teaspoon sugar

1½ pounds fresh wide rice noodles or dried rice noodles

5 tablespoons vegetable oil, divided

4 garlic cloves, thinly sliced

1 bunch Chinese broccoli (gai lan), stems sliced diagonally into ½-inch pieces, leaves cut into bite-size pieces

2 large eggs, beaten

1. In a mixing bowl, stir together the dark soy, cornstarch, 1 teaspoon of fish sauce, salt, and a pinch of white pepper. Add the beef slices and toss to coat. Set aside to marinate for 10 minutes.
2. In another bowl, stir together the oyster sauce, light soy, remaining 1 teaspoon of fish sauce, and sugar. Set aside.
3. If using fresh rice noodles, rinse them under hot water to keep them separated, and set aside. If using dried rice noodles, cook them according to package instructions, drain, and set aside.
4. Heat a wok over medium-high heat until a drop of water sizzles and evaporates on contact. Pour in 2 tablespoons of oil and swirl to coat the base of the wok. Using tongs, transfer the beef to the wok and reserve the marinade. Sear the beef against the wok for 2 to 3 minutes, until it's brown and a seared crust develops. Return the beef to the marinade bowl and stir in the oyster sauce mixture.

5. Add 2 more tablespoons of oil and stir-fry the garlic for 30 seconds. Add the Chinese broccoli stems and stir-fry for 45 seconds, keeping everything moving to prevent the garlic from burning.
6. Push the broccoli stems to the sides of the wok, leaving the bottom of the wok empty. Add the remaining 1 tablespoon of oil and scramble the eggs in the well, then toss them together.
7. Add the noodles, sauce, and beef, and toss and flip quickly to combine all of the ingredients, stir-frying for 30 more seconds. Add the broccoli leaves and stir-fry for 30 seconds more, or until the leaves begin to wilt. Return to a platter and serve immediately.

SERVING TIP: For all of you hot sauce freaks out there, sriracha is awesome over these noodles!

Chicken Chow Mein

SERVES 4 ; PREP TIME: 15 MINUTES ; COOK TIME: 15 MINUTES

This is a classic favorite featuring crispy, crunchy thin noodles tossed with a savory combination of chicken and vegetables. When making this dish, it's important to buy thin Hong Kong–style egg noodles, either dry or fresh. Change up the vegetables to what you have on hand. Snow peas, red bell peppers, carrots, and celery all work well in this dish.

½ pound fresh thin Hong Kong–style egg noodles

1½ tablespoons sesame oil, divided

2 teaspoons Shaoxing rice wine

2 teaspoons light soy sauce

Ground white pepper

½ pound chicken thighs, sliced into thin strips

¼ cup low-sodium chicken broth

2 teaspoons dark soy sauce

2 teaspoons oyster sauce

2 teaspoons cornstarch

4 tablespoons vegetable oil, divided

3 heads baby bok choy, cut into bite-sized pieces

2 garlic cloves, finely minced

1 large handful (2 to 3 ounces) mung bean sprouts

1. Bring a pot of water to a boil and cook the noodles according to package instructions. Reserve 1 cup of the cooking water and drain the noodles in a colander. Rinse the noodles with cold water and drizzle in 1 tablespoon of sesame oil. Toss to coat and set aside.
2. In a mixing bowl, combine the rice wine, light soy, and a pinch of white pepper. Toss the chicken pieces to coat and marinate for 10 minutes. In a small bowl, stir together the chicken broth, dark soy, remaining ½ tablespoon of sesame oil, oyster sauce, and cornstarch. Set aside.
3. Heat a wok over medium-high heat until a drop of water sizzles and evaporates on contact. Pour in 3 tablespoons of vegetable oil and swirl to coat the base of the wok. Add the noodles in one layer and fry for 2 to 3 minutes, or until they are golden brown. Flip the noodles over carefully and fry on the other side for 2 more minutes, or until the noodles are crispy and brown, and have formed into a loose cake. Transfer to a paper towel–lined plate and set aside.
4. Add the remaining 1 tablespoon of vegetable oil and stir-fry the chicken and marinade for 2 to 3 minutes, until the chicken is no longer pink and the marinade has evaporated.

Add the bok choy and garlic, stir-frying until the bok choy stems are tender, about another minute.

5. Pour in the sauce and toss to combine with the chicken and bok choy.
6. Return the noodles and, using a scooping and lifting motion, toss the noodles with the chicken and vegetables for about 2 minutes, until coated with the sauce. If the noodles seem a bit dry, add a tablespoon or so of the reserved cooking water as you toss. Add the bean sprouts and stir-fry, lifting and scooping for 1 more minute.
7. Transfer to a platter and serve hot.

Beef Lo Mein

SERVES 4 ; PREP TIME: 15 MINUTES ; COOK TIME: 20 MINUTES

Lo mein . . . chow mein . . . what's the difference? Well, chow mein is a dish made of savory toppings tossed into a nest of crispy, crunchy fried noodles. Lo mein is dish of softer, thicker noodles tossed with stir-fried toppings and more sauce. We think of it this way: "Chow" means fried whereas "lo" means poured or mixed with sauce. And of course, "mein" means long noodles.

½ pound fresh lo mein egg noodles

2 tablespoons sesame oil, divided

2 tablespoons Shaoxing rice wine

2 tablespoons cornstarch, divided

2 tablespoons dark soy sauce

Ground white pepper

½ pound beef sirloin tips, sliced across the grain into thin strips

3 tablespoons vegetable oil, divided

2 peeled fresh ginger slices, each about the size of a quarter

Kosher salt

½ red bell pepper, sliced into thin strips

1 cup snow peas, strings removed

2 garlic cloves, finely minced

2 cups mung bean sprouts

1. Bring a pot of water to a boil and cook the noodles according to package instructions. Reserve ½ cup of the cooking water and drain the noodles in a colander. Rinse the noodles under cold water and shake to drain excess water. Drizzle the noodles with 1 tablespoon of sesame oil and toss to coat. Set aside.
2. In a mixing bowl, stir together the rice wine, 2 teaspoons of cornstarch, dark soy, and a generous pinch of white pepper. Add the beef and toss to coat. Set aside for 10 minutes to marinate.
3. Heat a wok over medium-high heat until a drop of water sizzles and evaporates on contact. Pour in the vegetable oil and swirl to coat the base of the wok. Season the oil by adding the ginger and a small pinch of salt. Allow the ginger to sizzle in the oil for about 30 seconds, swirling gently. Add the beef, reserving the marinade, and sear against the wok for 2 to 3 minutes. Toss and flip the beef, stir-frying for 1 more minute, or until no longer pink. Transfer to a bowl and set aside.

4. Add the remaining 1 tablespoon of vegetable oil and stir-fry the bell pepper, tossing and flipping for 2 to 3 minutes, until tender. Add the snow peas and garlic, stir-frying for another minute, or until the garlic is fragrant.
5. Push all of the ingredients to the sides of the wok and pour in the remaining 1 tablespoon of sesame oil, reserved marinade, remaining 4 teaspoons of cornstarch, and ¼ cup of the reserved cooking water. Stir together and bring to a boil. Return the beef to the wok and toss to combine with the vegetables for 1 to 2 minutes, until the sauce becomes thick and glossy.
6. Toss the lo mein noodles with the beef and vegetables until the noodles are coated with the sauce. Add the bean sprouts and toss to combine. Remove and discard the ginger. Transfer to a platter and serve.

SUBSTITUTION TIP: Make our favorite "combination" lo mein by adding a mixture of stir-fried shrimp, chicken, beef, and pork.

Dan Dan Noodles

SERVES 4 ; PREP TIME: 20 MINUTES ; COOK TIME: 10 MINUTES

If you think of these noodles as a spicy, rich, Chinese version of pasta with Bolognese ragù, you're not wrong. Dan dan noodles are the most famous street food in the Sichuan province. Dan dan are what the merchants call their bundles attached to long poles they balance on their shoulders.

¾ pound thin wheat noodles

4 ounces ground pork

4 tablespoons vegetable oil, divided

2 tablespoons Shaoxing rice wine, divided

Kosher salt

¼ cup light soy sauce

2 tablespoons smooth peanut butter

1 tablespoon black vinegar

3 garlic cloves, finely minced

2 teaspoons light brown sugar

1 teaspoon Sichuan peppercorns, toasted and ground (use less as desired)

1-inch piece fresh ginger, peeled and finely minced

1 tablespoon fermented black beans, rinsed and chopped

2 small heads baby bok choy, coarsely chopped

2 tablespoons Fried Chili Oil

½ cup finely chopped dry roasted peanuts

1. Bring a large pot of water to a boil and cook the noodles according to package instructions. Drain and rinse with cold water and set aside. Fill the pot with fresh water and bring to a boil on the stove top.
2. In a bowl, mix the pork with 1 tablespoon of vegetable oil, 1 tablespoon of rice wine, and a pinch of salt. Set aside to marinate for 10 minutes.
3. In a small bowl, whisk together the remaining 1 tablespoon of rice wine, light soy, peanut butter, black vinegar, garlic, brown sugar, Sichuan peppercorns, ginger, and black beans. Set aside.
4. Heat a wok over medium-high heat until a drop of water sizzles and evaporates on contact. Pour in 2 tablespoons of vegetable oil and swirl to coat the base of the wok. Add the pork and stir-fry for 4 to 6 minutes, until browned and slightly crispy. Pour in the sauce mixture and toss to combine, simmering for 1 minute. Transfer to a clean bowl and set aside.

5. Wipe out the wok and add the remaining 1 tablespoon of vegetable oil. Quickly stir-fry the bok choy for 1 to 2 minutes, until just wilted and tender. Add to the pork bowl and stir together.
6. To assemble, dunk the noodles in the boiling water for 30 seconds to reheat. Drain and divide them among 4 deep bowls. Top each bowl with the pork mixture and drizzle with the chili oil. Top with the chopped peanuts and serve.

SUBSTITUTION TIP: Traditional dan dan noodles are made with Chinese sesame paste, not peanut butter. However, sesame paste is harder to find than peanut butter, but if you do manage to locate it, try that instead.

Chinese Birthday Noodles

SERVES 4 ; PREP TIME: 10 MINUTES ; COOK TIME: 10 MINUTES

Chinese families like to serve noodles at birthday celebrations to symbolize wishes for long life. Terri's mom makes awesome birthday noodles, but she rarely follows a recipe, so we've had to approximate the best we can. Dried Chinese egg noodles are great to keep in the pantry when the need for noodles arises. If you have an Asian market nearby, pick up a few packages. Amazon also can keep you stocked if you live in an area where Asian groceries are scarce.

¾ pound egg noodles

3 tablespoons sesame oil, divided

2 tablespoons vegetable oil

6 to 8 fresh shiitake mushrooms, stems removed and caps thinly sliced

½ pound medium shrimp (U41–50), peeled and deveined

1 shallot, thinly sliced

Kosher salt

4 ounces char shiu (Chinese barbecue pork), sliced into thin strips

½ cup frozen edamame beans, shelled and thawed

1 tablespoon light soy sauce

2 teaspoons Shaoxing rice wine

4 scallions, trimmed, white and green parts thinly sliced

3 tablespoons coarsely chopped fresh cilantro

1. Bring a pot of water to a boil and cook the noodles according to package instructions. Drain and rinse the noodles under cold water. Drizzle the noodles with 1 tablespoon of sesame oil and set aside.
2. Heat a wok over medium-high heat until a drop of water sizzles and evaporates on contact. Pour in the vegetable oil and swirl to coat the base of the wok. Add the mushrooms and toss to coat with the oil. Let the mushrooms sit against the wok and sear for 1 to 2 minutes. Toss and flip the mushrooms around for another 30 seconds, or until golden brown.
3. Add the shrimp and shallot and toss with the mushrooms. Stir-fry for 2 to 3 minutes, until the shrimp turns opaque and pink. Season with a pinch of salt. Add the char shui and edamame, tossing and flipping until heated through, about another minute. Drizzle in the light soy and rice wine and toss to coat.
4. Add the scallions and cilantro, reserving a small bit of each for garnish, and toss until the cilantro wilts slightly. Add the noodles and another pinch of salt. Toss and scoop, lifting upward to separate the noodle strands and combine with the shrimp and vegetables.

5. Transfer to a platter and drizzle with the remaining 2 tablespoons of sesame oil. Garnish with the reserved scallions and cilantro. Serve immediately. Happy Birthday!

VARIATION TIP: Char siu can be purchased at any Chinese restaurant or market, but for this "kitchen sink" recipe, just add what you have on hand and toss it all together with the noodles. Scrambled eggs, chopped vegetables, leftover proteins . . . you name it.

Beef Noodle Soup

SERVES 4 ; PREP TIME: 15 MINUTES ; COOK TIME: 20 MINUTES

You get home from work and you're craving beef noodle soup but don't have two hours to slowly braise the beef. Here is a quick version that's perfect for those days. We switched the stew meat for sirloin tips, cut the meat into thin strips, then tenderized with baking soda. These two changes will help the meat cook quickly and still give great flavor.

¾ pound beef sirloin tips, thinly sliced across the grain

2 teaspoons baking soda

4 tablespoons Shaoxing rice wine, divided

4 tablespoons light soy sauce, divided

2 teaspoons cornstarch, divided

1 teaspoon sugar

Kosher salt

Freshly ground black pepper

3 tablespoons vegetable oil, divided

2 teaspoons Chinese five spice powder

4 peeled fresh ginger slices, each about the size of a quarter

2 garlic cloves, peeled and smashed

4 cups beef broth

½ pound dried Chinese noodles (any type)

2 baby bok choy heads, quartered

1 tablespoon Scallion-Ginger Oil

1. In a small bowl, toss the beef with the baking soda and let it sit for 5 minutes. Rinse the beef and pat dry with paper towels. In another bowl, toss the beef with 1 tablespoon of rice wine, 1 tablespoon of light soy, 1 teaspoon of cornstarch, the sugar, and a pinch each of salt and pepper. Marinate for 10 minutes.
2. In a glass measuring cup, mix the remaining 3 tablespoons of rice wine, 3 tablespoons of light soy, and 1 teaspoon of cornstarch and set aside.
3. Heat a wok over medium-high heat until a drop of water sizzles and evaporates on contact. Pour in 2 tablespoons of vegetable oil and swirl to coat the base of the wok. Add the beef and five spice powder and cook for 3 to 4 minutes, tossing occasionally, until slightly browned. Transfer the beef to a clean bowl and set aside.
4. Wipe the wok clean and return it to medium heat. Add the remaining 1 tablespoon of vegetable oil and swirl to coat the base of the wok. Add the ginger, garlic, and a pinch of salt to season the oil. Allow the ginger and garlic to sizzle in the oil for about 10 seconds, swirling gently.

5. Pour in the soy sauce mixture and bring to a boil. Pour in the broth and return to a boil. Reduce to a simmer and return the beef to the wok. Simmer for 10 minutes.
6. Meanwhile, bring a large pot of water to a boil over high heat. Add the noodles and cook per package instructions. Using a wok skimmer, scoop out the noodles and drain. Add the bok choy to the boiling water and cook for 2 to 3 minutes, until bright green and tender. Scoop out the bok choy and place in a bowl. Using tongs, toss the noodles with the scallion-ginger oil to coat. Divide the noodles and bok choy into soup bowls.
7. Remove the garlic and ginger from the soup and discard. Divide the meat among the soup bowls, top with the broth, and serve.

PREP TIP: If you have any stir-fried beef left over from another recipe, this is a great way to morph it into a noodle soup dish.

Beef Chow Fun

SERVES 4 ; PREP TIME: 15 MINUTES ; COOK TIME: 10 MINUTES

Wok-fried rice noodles with thin slices of beef—sounds incredibly fun, no? "Fun" is actually the Chinese word for flat rice noodles, which can be found fresh at Asian markets. If they are not available in your area, however, do not worry. You can still make a delicious and satisfying dish using dried rice noodles; just get the widest ones you can find.

¼ cup Shaoxing rice wine

¼ cup light soy sauce

2 tablespoons cornstarch

1½ tablespoons dark soy sauce

1½ tablespoons dark soy sauce

½ teaspoon sugar

Ground white pepper

¾ pound flank steak or sirloin tips, cut across the grain into ⅛-inch-thick slices

1½ pounds fresh wide rice noodles or ¾ pound dried

2 tablespoons sesame oil, divided

3 tablespoons vegetable oil, divided

4 peeled fresh ginger slices, each about the size of a quarter

Kosher salt

8 scallions, halved lengthwise and cut into 3-inch pieces

2 cups fresh mung bean sprouts

1. In a mixing bowl, stir together the rice wine, light soy, cornstarch, dark soy, sugar, and a pinch of white pepper. Add the beef and toss to coat. Set aside to marinate for at least 10 minutes.
2. Bring a large pot of water to a boil and cook the rice noodles according to package instructions. Reserve 1 cup of the cooking water and drain the rest. Rinse with cold water and drizzle with 1 tablespoon of sesame oil. Set aside.
3. Heat a wok over medium-high heat until a drop of water sizzles and evaporates on contact. Pour in 2 tablespoons of vegetable oil and swirl to coat the base of the wok. Season the oil by adding the ginger and a pinch of salt. Allow the ginger to sizzle in the oil for about 30 seconds, swirling gently.
4. Using tongs, add the beef to the wok and reserve the marinating liquid. Sear the beef against the wok for 2 to 3 minutes, or until a seared, browned crust develops. Toss and flip the beef around the wok for 1 more minute. Transfer to a clean bowl and set aside.
5. Add 1 more tablespoon of vegetable oil and stir-fry the scallions for 30 seconds, or until soft. Add the noodles and lift in a scooping upward motion to help separate the noodles

if they have stuck together. Add the cooking water, 1 tablespoon at a time, if the noodles have really glued themselves together.

6. Return the beef to the wok and toss to combine with the noodles. Pour in the reserved marinade and toss for 30 seconds to 1 minute, or until the sauce thickens and coats the noodles and they turn a deep, rich brown color. If you need to, add 1 tablespoon of the reserved cooking water to thin out the sauce. Add the bean sprouts and toss until just heated through, about 1 minute. Remove the ginger and discard.
7. Transfer to a platter and drizzle with the remaining 1 tablespoon of sesame oil. Serve hot.

SUBSTITUTION TIP: Beef is a classic protein for chow fun dishes, but sliced boneless, skinless chicken thighs or shrimp work well if you're searching for something different and out of the ordinary.

SAUCES, SNACKS, AND SWEETS

XO Sauce

MAKES 2½ CUPS ; PREP TIME: 15 MINUTES ; COOK TIME: 10 MINUTES

XO sauce originated from Hong Kong and is rich, spicy, savory, and unbelievably delicious as a condiment to replace chili oils and dipping sauces. Sometimes, when we're hungry but not in the mood to fix up anything, a bowl of cooked noodles topped with XO sauce does the trick. Dried scallops are expensive but absolutely necessary for this sauce; you can find them at Asian markets or online. When cooking this sauce, remember to open a window and turn on your exhaust fan, as the chilies can be overpowering.

2 cups large dried scallops

20 dried red chilies, stems removed

2 fresh red chilies, coarsely chopped

2 shallots, coarsely chopped

2 garlic cloves, coarsely chopped

½ cup small dried shrimp

3 slices bacon, minced

½ cup vegetable oil

1 tablespoon dark brown sugar

2 teaspoons Chinese five spice powder

2 tablespoons Shaoxing rice wine

1. In a large glass bowl, place the scallops and cover by an inch with boiling water. Soak for 10 minutes, or until the scallops are soft. Drain off all but 2 tablespoons of water and cover with plastic wrap. Microwave for 3 minutes. Set aside to cool slightly. Using your fingers, break the scallops up into smaller shreds, rubbing them together to loosen the scallops. Transfer to a food processor and pulse 10 to 15 times, or until the scallops are finely shredded. Transfer to a bowl and set aside.
2. In the food processor, combine the dried chilies, fresh chilies, shallots, and garlic. Pulse several times until the mixture forms a paste and looks finely minced. You may need to scrape down the sides as you go to keep everything uniform in size. Transfer the mixture to the scallop bowl and set aside.
3. Add the shrimp and bacon to the food processor and pulse a few times to finely mince.
4. Heat a wok over medium-high heat. Pour in the oil and swirl to coat the pan. Add the shrimp and bacon and cook for 1 to 2 minutes, until the bacon browns and becomes very crispy. Add the brown sugar and five spice powder and cook for 1 minute more, until the brown sugar caramelizes.
5. Add the scallop and chili-garlic mixture and cook for another 1 to 2 minutes, or until the garlic begins to caramelize. Carefully pour the rice wine down the sides of the wok and

cook for 2 to 3 minutes more, until evaporated. Be careful—at this point the oil may spatter from the wine.

6. Transfer the sauce to a bowl and cool. Once cooled, separate the sauce into smaller jars and cover. The XO sauce can keep in the refrigerator for up to 1 month.

VARIATION TIP: Consider making a vegetarian version by adding a variety of wild mushrooms such as chanterelle and lobster mushrooms, and dulse seaweed in place of the seafood and bacon.

Fried Chili Oil

MAKES ABOUT 1 CUP ; PREP TIME: 5 MINUTES ; COOK TIME: 5 MINUTES, PLUS COOLING TIME

If you like adding a deeply layered chili oil to your food as much as we do, try this one. It takes almost no time to make and can brighten any dish. Warning: It's addictive and you'll find yourself adding it to everything. For the bright red oil, you need Sichuan chili flakes, but play around and make it your own. For more heat, add a couple tablespoons more chili flakes or try using Korean chili flakes, which tend to be spicier than Sichuan chili flakes.

¼ cup Sichuan chili flakes

2 tablespoons white sesame seeds

1 star anise pod

1 cinnamon stick

1 teaspoon kosher salt

1 cup vegetable oil

1. In a heatproof glass or stainless-steel bowl, combine the chili flakes, sesame seeds, anise, cinnamon stick, and salt and stir. Set aside.
2. Pour the oil into a wok and heat over medium-high heat, until the cinnamon stick immediately sizzles when dipped in the oil. Once the oil is hot, remove the wok from the heat and carefully pour the hot oil over the spices. The mixture should sizzle as you pour and bubble up. Pour the oil slowly so it does not bubble over.
3. Allow the mixture to cool completely, about 20 minutes. Stir, transfer to an airtight jar, and refrigerate for up to 4 weeks.

VARIATION TIP: Lao gan ma, a well-loved chili oil from the Guizhou region in China, adds fried peanuts and tofu and other aromatic bits to the oil. It's a game changer. Make a simplified version by adding ¼ cup dry roasted peanuts to the hot oil and fry for 30 seconds before pouring into the spice mixture.

Plum Sauce

MAKES ABOUT 2 CUPS ; PREP TIME: 15 MINUTES ; COOK TIME: 1 HOUR

Fresh plum sauce is a revelation if you've only ever had the jarred sauce as a condiment for Chinese food. When the plums are at their peak, make multiple batches and process as you would jams or marmalade. One piece of advice: Don't peel the skins off the plums, as they give off a brilliant jewel color that can brighten any dish. If you like spice, add a pinch of cayenne pepper while cooking it down to give it a kick.

4 cups coarsely chopped plums (about 1½ pounds)

½ small yellow onion, chopped

½-inch fresh ginger slice, peeled

1 garlic clove, peeled and smashed

½ cup water

⅓ cup light brown sugar

¼ cup apple cider vinegar

½ teaspoon Chinese five spice powder

Kosher salt

1. In a wok, bring the plums, onion, ginger, garlic, and water to a boil over medium-high heat. Cover, reduce the heat to medium, and simmer, stirring occasionally, until the plums and onion are tender, about 20 minutes.
2. Transfer the mixture to a blender or food processor and blend until smooth. Return to the wok and stir in the sugar, vinegar, five spice powder, and a pinch of salt.
3. Turn the heat back to medium-high and bring to a boil, stirring frequently. Reduce the heat to low and simmer until the mixture reaches the consistency of applesauce, about 30 minutes.
4. Transfer to a clean jar and cool to room temperature. Refrigerate for up to a week or freeze for up to a month.

VARIATION TIP: Apple cider vinegar lends a sweet-tart flavor. If you want to turn up the tartness of the sauce, use unsweetened rice vinegar instead.

Hakka Spice Popcorn

SERVES 4 ; PREP TIME: 10 MINUTES ; COOK TIME: 10 MINUTES

We are popcorn fiends! We've done movie nights with every flavor of popcorn you can imagine. From truffle to Hakka spice popcorn, we love them all. Did you know that popping popcorn on the stove top is still the best way to make popcorn at home? And a wok is the best cookware for making popcorn. As the kernels pop, the large, fluffy pieces stay on top and allow the small kernels to keep rolling down to the bottom.

FOR THE SPICE BLEND

1 whole star anise, seeds removed and husks discarded

6 green cardamom pods, seeds removed and husks discarded

4 whole cloves

4 black peppercorns

1 teaspoon coriander seeds

1 teaspoon fennel seeds

1 teaspoon ground cinnamon

1 teaspoon ground ginger

½ teaspoon ground turmeric

⅛ teaspoon ground cayenne pepper

FOR THE POPCORN

2 tablespoons vegetable oil

½ cup popcorn kernels

Kosher salt

TO MAKE THE SPICE BLEND

1. In a small sauté pan or skillet, combine the star anise seeds, cardamom seeds, cloves, peppercorns, coriander seeds, and fennel seeds. Heat the skillet over medium heat and gently shake and swirl the spices around the pan. Toast the spices for 5 to 6 minutes, or until you can smell the spices and they start to pop.
2. Remove the pan from the heat and transfer the spices to a mortar and pestle or spice grinder. Cool the spices for 2 minutes before grinding. Grind the spices to a fine powder and transfer to a small bowl.
3. Add the ground cinnamon, ginger, turmeric, and cayenne pepper and stir to combine. Set aside.

TO MAKE THE POPCORN

4. Heat a wok over medium-high heat until it just begins to smoke. Pour in the vegetable oil and ghee and swirl to coat the wok. Add 2 popcorn kernels to the wok and cover. Once

they pop, add the rest of the kernels and cover. Shake constantly until the popping stops and remove from the heat.

5. Transfer the popcorn to a large paper bag. Add 2 generous pinches of kosher salt and 1½ tablespoons of the spice blend. Fold the bag closed and shake! Pour into a large bowl and enjoy immediately.

VARIATION TIP: The spice blends are limited only by your imagination and spice cabinet. Curry powder, garam masala, furikake seasoning . . . all are delicious on popcorn!

Black Bean Sauce

MAKES ABOUT 2 CUPS ; PREP TIME: 10 MINUTES ; COOK TIME: 10 MINUTES

Black bean sauce is a powerful flavor boost in many stir-fry recipes. It goes well with just about any type of seafood, vegetable, or protein. Even the most boring ingredients can be transformed into a flavorful dish thanks to the umami punch from the fermented black beans. Although you can use the jarred variety instead, there are no added sugars, shelf stabilizers, or additives in this homemade version.

½ cup fermented black beans

1 cup vegetable oil, divided

1 large shallot, finely minced

3 tablespoons peeled and minced fresh ginger

4 scallions, thinly sliced

6 garlic cloves, finely minced

½ cup Shaoxing rice wine

1. Put the black beans in a small bowl, cover with hot water, and let soak for 10 minutes to soften. Drain and coarsely chop the beans.
2. Heat a wok over medium-high heat. Pour in ¼ cup of oil and swirl to coat the pan. Add the shallot, ginger, scallions, and garlic and stir-fry for 1 minute, or until the mixture has softened.
3. Add the black beans and rice wine. Lower the heat to medium and cook for 3 to 4 minutes, until the mixture is reduced by half.
4. Transfer the mixture to an airtight container and cool to room temperature. Pour the remaining ¾ cup of oil over the top and cover tightly. Keep in the refrigerator until ready to use.
5. This fresh bean sauce will keep in the refrigerator in an airtight container for up to a month. If you wish to keep it for longer, freeze it in smaller portions.

PREP TIP: Blend the black bean sauce to make it smoother and less chunky.

Scallion-Ginger Oil

MAKES ABOUT 2 CUPS ; PREP TIME: 5 MINUTES ; COOK TIME: 5 MINUTES, PLUS COOLING TIME

Scallion-ginger oil is one of our go-tos when we need a little more flavor for just about anything. Add it hot to congee, noodles, scrambled eggs, proteins, and vegetables; add it cold to salads. For even more flavor, add a minced fresh chili or a couple minced garlic cloves.

1½ cups thinly sliced scallions

1 tablespoon peeled and finely minced fresh ginger

1 teaspoon kosher salt

1 cup vegetable oil

1. In a heatproof glass or stainless-steel bowl, toss the scallions, ginger, and salt. Set aside.
2. Pour the oil into a wok and heat over medium-high heat, until a piece of scallion green immediately sizzles when dropped in the oil. Once the oil is hot, remove the wok from the heat and carefully pour the hot oil over the scallions and ginger. The mixture should sizzle as you pour and bubble up. Pour the oil slowly so it does not bubble over.
3. Allow the mixture to cool completely, about 20 minutes. Stir, transfer to an airtight jar, and refrigerate for up to 2 weeks.

PREP TIP: Throw the scallions and ginger in a food processor to speed up the prep time.

Tea-Soaked Eggs

SERVES 4 ; PREP TIME: 1 DAY ; COOK TIME: 40 MINUTES

These hard-boiled eggs, cracked with the shell left on and then soaked in a flavorful tea and spice mixture, are as beautiful as they are delicious. Because the eggs can become rubbery during the soaking process, we show you how to cook them to achieve the perfect outcome: a slightly soft center and no green ring.

2 cups water

¾ cup dark soy sauce

6 peeled fresh ginger slices, each about the size of a quarter

2 whole star anise

2 cinnamon sticks

6 whole cloves

1 teaspoon fennel seeds

1 teaspoon Sichuan peppercorns or black peppercorns

1 teaspoon sugar

5 decaf black tea bags

8 large eggs, at room temperature

1. In a saucepan, bring the water to a boil. Add the dark soy, ginger, anise, cinnamon sticks, cloves, fennel seeds, peppercorns, and sugar. Cover the pot and reduce the heat to a simmer; cook for 20 minutes. Turn off the heat and add the tea bags. Steep the tea for 10 minutes. Strain the tea through a fine-mesh sieve into a large heatproof measuring cup and allow to cool while you cook the eggs.
2. Fill a large bowl with ice and water to create an ice bath for the eggs and set aside. In a wok, bring enough water to cover the eggs by about an inch to a boil. Gently lower the eggs into the water, reduce the heat to a simmer, and cook for 9 minutes. Remove the eggs with a slotted spoon and transfer to the ice bath until cool.
3. Remove the eggs from the ice bath. Tap the eggs with the back of a spoon to crack the shells so the marinade can seep in between the cracks, but gently enough to leave the shells on. The shells should end up looking like a mosaic. Place the eggs in a large jar (at least 32 ounces) and cover them with the marinade. Store them in the refrigerator for at least 24 hours or up to a week. Remove the eggs from the marinade when ready to serve.

SUBSTITUTION TIP: Don't have all the whole spices on hand? A couple teaspoons of Chinese five spice powder can be substituted.

Steamed Scallion Buns

MAKES 8 BUNS ; PREP TIME: 90 MINUTES ; COOK TIME: 20 MINUTES

The dough for these buns is the same as that used to make steamed buns for steamed baos, but we twist these into an interesting presentation, so make these when you need to impress or celebrate a special occasion. The hardest part of the recipe is the proofing time; even though the shaping of the buns look hard, it's actually very easy.

¾ cup whole milk, at room temperature

1 tablespoon sugar

1 teaspoon active dry yeast

2 cups all-purpose flour

1 teaspoon baking powder

¾ teaspoon kosher salt, divided

2 tablespoons sesame oil, divided

2 teaspoons Chinese five spice powder, divided

6 scallions, thinly sliced

1. In a liquid measuring cup, stir together the milk, sugar, and yeast. Set aside for 5 minutes to activate the yeast.
2. In a large mixing bowl or using a stand mixer with a dough hook attachment on low, stir the flour, baking powder, and ¼ teaspoon of salt to combine. Pour in the milk mixture and mix for 30 seconds. Increase the speed to high and mix for 5 minutes, until a soft, elastic dough forms, or 6 to 8 minutes by hand. Turn the dough out onto a work surface and knead a few times by hand until smooth. Place in a bowl and cover with a towel to rest for 10 minutes.
3. Cut the dough in half. With a rolling pin, roll one piece out into a rectangle, 15 by 18 inches. Brush 1 tablespoon of sesame oil over the dough. Season with 1 teaspoon of five spice powder and ¼ teaspoon of salt. Sprinkle with half the scallions and press gently into the dough.
4. Roll the dough up starting from the long edge as you would a cinnamon roll. Cut the rolled log into 8 equal pieces. To shape the bun, take 2 pieces and stack them one on top of the other on their sides, so the cut sides are facing out.
5. Use a chopstick to press down in the center of the stack; this will push out the filling slightly. Remove the chopstick. Using your fingers, pull the two ends of the dough out slightly to stretch, and then coil the ends underneath the middle, pinching the ends together.
6. Place the bun on a 3-inch square of parchment paper and set inside a steamer basket to proof. Repeat the shaping process with the remaining dough, making sure there is at least 2 inches of space between the buns. You can use a second steamer basket if you

need more room. You should have 8 twisted buns. Cover the baskets with plastic wrap and let rise for 1 hour, or until doubled in size.

7. Pour about 2 inches of water into the wok and place the steamer baskets in the wok. The water level should come above the bottom rim of the steamer by ¼ to ½ inch but not so high that it touches the bottom of the basket. Cover the baskets with the steamer basket lid and bring the water to a boil over medium-high heat.
8. Reduce the heat to medium and steam for 15 minutes, adding more water to the wok if needed. Turn off the heat and keep the baskets covered for 5 more minutes. Transfer the buns to a platter and serve.

VARIATION TIP: Add some chopped ham or cooked bacon bits to the scallions for an extra savory twist.

Steamed Milk Custard

SERVES 4 ; PREP TIME: 5 MINUTES ; COOK TIME: 30 MINUTES

A rich meal needs a sweet but light finish at the end for dessert. Might we suggest these steamed milk custards? They are super easy to make and can be served warm or chilled, so make them a day ahead and keep them in the refrigerator until you are ready to serve. If cooking from chilled, add 5 minutes to the cooking time.

1¼ cups whole milk

1 cup half-and-half

⅓ cup sugar

1 teaspoon vanilla extract

3 large egg whites

1 ripe mango, seeded and diced

1. In a medium saucepan, stir together the milk, half-and-half, and sugar over medium heat. Warm the mixture, stirring occasionally, until the sugar has dissolved, about 5 minutes. Do not let the mixture boil or simmer. Turn off the heat and stir in the vanilla. Set aside.
2. In a mixing bowl, beat the egg whites until frothy. Continue whisking while carefully pouring in the milk and stir to combine.
3. Pour the custard through a fine-mesh strainer into another bowl and then divide the custard among 4 (6-ounce) ramekins or custard cups. Cover the ramekins with aluminum foil.
4. Rinse a bamboo steamer basket and its lid under cold water and place it in the wok. Pour in 2 inches of water, or until it comes above the bottom rim of the steamer by ¼ to ½ inch, but not so much that it touches the bottom of the basket. Place the ramekins in the steamer basket.
5. Cover the basket and steam over medium-high heat for 8 minutes. Turn off the heat and let the custards sit in place for another 10 minutes before removing from the steamer. The custards will appear set, with a slight wobble.
6. Transfer to a cooling rack and cool to room temperature before chilling in the refrigerator to set. Serve chilled, topped with diced mango.

Steamed Almond Sponge Cake

SERVES 4 ; PREP TIME: 10 MINUTES ; COOK TIME: 25 MINUTES

Soft, tender, spongy almond cake is such a treat when it rolls by on the dim sum cart. It's a very simple cake to put together, so don't wait for special occasions to make it. The trick is to whip the egg whites to a meringue and fold it into the cake batter. Don't overmix the cake or else it won't rise and develop that wonderful bouncy, spongy texture.

Nonstick cooking spray

1 cup cake flour, sifted

1 teaspoon baking powder

¼ teaspoon kosher salt

5 large eggs, separated

¾ cup sugar, divided

1 teaspoon almond extract

½ teaspoon cream of tartar

1. Line an 8-inch cake pan with parchment paper. Lightly spray the parchment with nonstick cooking spray and set aside.
2. Into a bowl, sift the cake flour, baking powder, and salt together.
3. In a stand mixer or hand mixer on medium, beat the egg yolks with ½ cup of sugar and the almond extract for about 3 minutes, until pale and thick. Add the flour mixture and mix until just combined. Set aside.
4. Clean the whisk and in another clean bowl, whip the egg whites with the cream of tartar until frothy. While the mixer is running, continue to whisk the whites while gradually adding the remaining ¼ cup of sugar. Beat for 4 to 5 minutes, until the whites turn shiny and develop stiff peaks.
5. Fold the egg whites into the cake batter and gently combine until the egg whites are incorporated. Transfer the batter to the prepared cake pan.
6. Rinse a bamboo steamer basket and its lid under cold water and place it in the wok. Pour in 2 inches of water, or until it comes above the bottom rim of the steamer by ¼ to ½ inch, but not so much that it touches the bottom of the basket. Set the center pan in the steamer basket.
7. Bring the water to a boil over high heat. Place the cover on the steamer basket and turn the heat down to medium. Steam the cake for 25 minutes, or until a toothpick inserted into the center comes out clean.
8. Transfer the cake to a wire cooling rack and cool for 10 minutes. Turn the cake out onto the rack and remove the parchment paper. Invert the cake back onto a serving plate so that it is right side up. Slice into 8 wedges and serve warm.

SERVING TIP: Though not necessary to garnish the cake, you can serve it with a dollop of slightly sweetened whipped cream and sprinkle with toasted sliced almonds.

Chrysanthemum and Peach Tong Sui (Dessert Soup)

SERVES 4 ; PREP TIME: 5 MINUTES ; COOK TIME: 15 MINUTES

Tong sui means sugar water. This simple soup can be served hot in the winter months and cold in the summer months. In Hong Kong, there is a fourth meal enjoyed late in the evening, sometimes into the wee hours of the morning—a midnight snack if you will. Siu yeh (small things), or late-night snack, is a lovely practice, much like afternoon tea in Great Britain, and tong sui makes a great finish to siu yeh.

3 cups water

¾ cup granulated sugar

¼ cup light brown sugar

2-inch fresh ginger piece, peeled and smashed

1 tablespoon dried chrysanthemum buds

2 large yellow peaches, peeled, pitted, and sliced into 8 wedges each

1. In a wok over high heat, bring the water to a boil, then lower the heat to medium-low and add the granulated sugar, brown sugar, ginger, and chrysanthemum buds. Stir gently to dissolve the sugars. Add the peaches.
2. Simmer gently for 10 to 15 minutes, or until the peaches are tender. They may impart a beautiful rosy color to the soup. Discard the ginger and divide the soup and peaches into bowls and serve.

VARIATION TIP: Let your creativity go wild . . . infuse the soup with citrus peel, edible rose petals, jasmine tea, star anise pods, or cinnamon sticks, just to name a few.

Sugar Egg Puffs

MAKES 8 PUFFS ; PREP TIME: 10 MINUTES ; COOK TIME: 20 MINUTES

These Sugar Egg Puffs are made with a dough similar to that for a fried doughnut or churro; however, their texture is much more delicate because of the higher egg-to-flour ratio. These puffs are best right out of the oil.

½ cup water

2 teaspoons unsalted butter

¼ cup sugar, divided

Kosher salt

½ cup all-purpose unbleached flour

3 cups vegetable oil

2 large eggs, beaten

1. In a small saucepan, heat the water, butter, 2 teaspoons of sugar, and a pinch of salt over medium-high heat. Bring to a boil and stir in the flour. Continue stirring the flour with a wooden spoon until the mixture looks like mashed potatoes and a thin film of dough has developed on the bottom of the pan. Turn off the heat and transfer the dough to a large mixing bowl. Cool the dough for about 5 minutes, stirring occasionally.
2. While the dough cools, pour the oil into the wok; the oil should be about 1 to 1½ inches deep. Bring the oil to 375°F over medium-high heat. You can tell the oil is ready when you dip the end of a wooden spoon in and the oil bubbles and sizzles around the spoon.
3. Pour the beaten eggs into the dough in two batches, vigorously stirring the eggs into the dough before adding the next batch. When all the eggs have been incorporated, the batter should look satiny and shiny.
4. Using 2 tablespoons, scoop the batter with one and use the other to gently nudge the batter off the spoon into the hot oil. Let the puffs fry for 8 to 10 minutes, flipping often, until the puffs swell to 3 times their original size and turn golden brown and crispy.
5. Using a wok skimmer, transfer the puffs to a paper towel–lined plate and cool for 2 to 3 minutes. Place the remaining sugar in a bowl and toss the puffs in it. Serve warm.

CPSIA information can be obtained
at www.ICGtesting.com
Printed in the USA
LVHW050136110622
721005LV00009B/469